Praise for *The Culture Secret*

"One of the most important things I have observed is seeing how important getting the culture right really is to building great companies. The best thing you can do for growing your business is reading *The Culture Secret*. Doc nailed it."

—Larry Benet, the "Connector," and founder of SANG (Speakers and Authors Networking Group)

"We were stuck—but now we have one of America's fastest-growing companies. It's fun—we are all engaged and reaching our full potential, taking it to the next level. Read *The Culture Secret* and see what it can do for you, your employees, and your company. Doc's the guru."

—Ali Behnam, managing partner and cofounder of Riviera Partners

"Doc's recipe is simple: you must believe that by creating the right culture and empowering your team, your company *will* reach its potential. *The Culture Secret* is the what, why, and how of creating winning organizations that endure."

—Michael A. Morell, managing partner and cofounder of Riviera Partners

"Your business culture determines your success more than any other factor, and this excellent book shows you how to identify it, shape it, improve it, and promote it to everyone."

—Brian Tracy, author of *How the Best Leaders Lead*

"We saw firsthand what Dr. Vik has done to empower people at the companies he's worked with, and it is nothing short of amazing. Now he shares his road map in *The Culture Secret*. If you are a leader, you would do well to heed the Doc's clear, concise, and powerful messages."

—Adrian Gostick and Chester Elton, *New York Times* bestselling authors of *All In* and *The Carrot Principle*

"*The Culture Secret* provides business leaders the most up-to-date, comprehensive, and effective approach to creating an exceptional corporate culture. When it comes to business success, culture is king, and I highly recommend that every manager and leader read this book."

—Jon Gordon, bestselling author of *The Energy Bus* and
Soup: A Recipe to Nourish Your Team and Culture

"Learn from former Zappos coach Doc Vik on making corporate culture a part of your profitability and growth strategy."

—Jeanne Bliss, author of *I Love You More Than My Dog:
Five Decisions That Drive Extreme Customer Loyalty in
Good Times and Bad*

"When it comes to creating a world-class culture, Dr. Vik has the chops, and he writes from deep experience. This book is chock-full of interesting anecdotes, enlightening illustrations, and how-to-do-it strategies. If you're tired of academic treatises and want practical, powerful ideas to supercharge your culture, read this book."

—Mark Sanborn, bestselling author of *The Fred Factor*
and *You Don't Need a Title to Be a Leader*

THE
CULTURE
SECRET

How to Empower People and Companies
No Matter What You Sell

DR. DAVID VIK

GREENLEAF
BOOK GROUP PRESS

Published by Greenleaf Book Group Press
Austin, Texas
www.greenleafbookgroup.com

Distributed by Greenleaf Book Group LLC
For ordering information or special discounts for bulk purchases, please contact Greenleaf Book Group LLC at PO Box 91869, Austin, TX 78709, 512.891.6100.

Design and composition by Greenleaf Book Group LLC
Cover design by Greenleaf Book Group LLC

Publisher's Cataloging-In-Publication Data
(Prepared by The Donohue Group, Inc.)

Vik, David.
    The culture secret : how to empower people and companies no matter what you sell / David Vik. -- 1st ed.

    p. ; cm.

    Issued also as an ebook.
    ISBN: 978-1-60832-402-6

    1. Employee empowerment. 2. Employee retention. 3. Corporate culture. I. Title.

HD50.5 .V55 2013
658.4/02   2012947768

Part of the Tree Neutral® program, which offsets the number of trees consumed in the production and printing of this book by taking proactive steps, such as planting trees in direct proportion to the number of trees used: www.treeneutral.com

TreeNeutral®

Printed in the United States of America on acid-free paper

12 13 14 15 16   10 9 8 7 6 5 4 3 2 1

First Edition

Dedication

A personal dedication to my family: To Lori, Victoria, Sam, and Chris for helping me to be the best I can be in helping others. To my two sisters, Kathy and Teri, who have both taught me so much. And to my two sets of parents, Doris and Bill, and Lyle and Barbara—for I would not be anything without loving parents.

Contents

Introduction

From 2005 through 2009 I was honored to be the "Coach" at Zappos.com, which started out to be an online shoe store, and I saw the amazing things people can and will do when they are part of something special. The employees brought their lives to the Next Level and took the company to the Next Level as well.

As the Coach at Zappos, I saw an opportunity to help create the best Culture on the planet. Why was that important? Well, for starters, selling shoes isn't really new or unique, and selling them online—where you couldn't see, feel, or touch them—was probably not the best business model in the world . . . at least when the company began. Because customers requested many sizes, we needed to have 20 pairs in stock just to sell one, and shoes went out of style relatively quickly. To be successful, we had to differentiate ourselves. Service and Experience was our North Star. We were set on delivering "WOW," which was the expression our customers used when they received Zappos products or interacted with Zappos employees.

Could we deliver the best service and create a WOW experience if our employees were unappreciated, un-empowered, or treated poorly? The answer was, plainly, no. We needed to align our Culture with what we wanted to deliver—the WOW! So we started with our employees; we worked to create the mind-set of winning while providing them the best service and experience and delivering the WOW. This allowed our employees to reciprocate and pass along the same service, experience, and WOW to our customers.

As Coach, even though I was part of the team within management, my focus was on working with the employees, the "players." It's like a professional sports team. Management mostly focuses on managing, making sure the seats are filled, that TV revenue is growing, and creating enthusiastic, long-term fans. But none of that will happen if the team's thoughts, decisions, and actions are not focused on winning. That's the reason a sports team has a Coach on the field: to coach the individual players and help empower them to reach their full potential. That, in turn, helps the team to reach its full potential.

When I arrived at Zappos, the first thing I did was to begin to create relationships with the employees. I had sign-up sheets and arranged for employees to meet with me for at least half an hour so I could get to know them better—where they were born, what happened to them after high school, where they lived, the details of their family; basically I got to know each of them as a person as well as their "deal." Before long the employees came to understand that by taking time to get to know them, I really cared about them, and I truly did. I got to know each employee as an individual—as a person with dreams, aspirations, and a life outside of the company—not just as an employee. That's just what we did at Zappos. We understood the value of *relationships*, and relationships eventually became one of our core values: Build Open and Honest Relationships With Communication. That was "how we rolled."

The result was that the employees felt like they mattered to everyone in the organization, which was the truth. The employees, in turn, focused on treating customers like they mattered.

I wrote this book for those of you who feel trapped in your jobs and want to go somewhere where you won't feel you're wasting your life for a paycheck. You would certainly give back and help your company reach its potential if you found a workplace that rewarded your contributions and helped you reach *your* potential. You deserve that better work environment, one that elevates your life and the lives of those around you.

I also wrote this book for CEOs, those in management, and business owners who want to create a dynamic culture that attracts and retains employees, who in turn will attract and retain customers. The ideas I share with you in this book are not based on my experience at Zappos alone. I founded a chiropractic clinic in 1982, and it, too, over 20-plus years, experienced phenomenal growth. (You'll read more about that in the Unique/WOW Factors section.) The clinic is where I learned that a culture founded on showing people that they matter—whether they're employees, customers, or other stakeholders—makes for a business that is unstoppable. I've demonstrated the same results in other industries as well, as I've helped health-care, Internet, and services-sector companies take it to the Next Level.

There are two parts to any Culture. The first part is its structure; the second part is the living, breathing people in it. The blueprint for the structure is composed of five key aspects: what the organization or company is doing and wants to do (Vision); why the organization or company is doing it (Purpose) and how it is going to be done or what fuels it (Business Model), together with what makes it stand out (Unique/WOW Factors) and what the company and employees care about, or value (Values). All of that is described in detail in the first half of the book. The second half covers how people function inside the structure, that is, their habits, routines, and commonalities like language, beliefs, thoughts, decisions, and actions, which are created by the Culture and aligned to it. So the second half of the book includes leadership, human empowerment, relationships with customers, brand, and the desired experience that is to be delivered. When we're inside a well-constructed and articulated Culture, we can, and should, focus on the people creating it, for they are the ones who will support, drive, and enhance an organization or company as it brings the Culture to life!

My hope, dream, and vision is that individuals, groups, teams, organizations, and those in management will implement the ideas, processes, and procedures in this book in order to take themselves, their personal lives, and their companies to the Next Level. My belief is that those people and companies will start attracting a great many others to do the same.

As you read on, please think about

What is
&
What could be

A GREAT CULTURE SHOULDN'T BE SO RARE

I was in my office at Zappos, when my phone rang, and the voice on the other end said, "Hi, this is Jonathan Schienberg, from CBS/60 Minutes." I thought it was a joke. But my phone's caller ID clearly showed that the call was coming from CBS.

Floored, I asked him, "What can I help you with?" He told me that Chester Elton and Adrian Gostick had referred him to me because he was filming a segment on corporate culture for 60 Minutes. They said I was the person to talk to about Culture and empowering employees. (Chester Elton and Adrian Gostick have written many books like The Carrot Principle and The Orange Revolution and are instrumental in beginning an acknowledgment and recognition revolution in the workplace.)

Jonathan said he would like to ask me some questions, but we got to talking about the incredible effects of a great Culture like Zappos', both within a company and in the personal lives of employees. An hour later, he had agreed to talk about scheduling a visit to do a separate segment just on Zappos, even though the filming season was wrapping up in a couple weeks.

I am forever grateful to Chester Elton and Adrian Gostick for telling Jonathan about me and Zappos and also grateful to Jonathan for switching his plans and actually understanding why it was important to focus on Zappos and its unique Culture.

However, it's a shame that a great Culture—which puts all of its efforts into the service and experience of the employees, customers, and vendors—is so rare that 60 Minutes would do a segment about it. Cultures like Zappos' should be the norm and not the exception in the corporate world of the Information Age. If it were, I am sure that a lot of people and companies would be much happier and that the world would be a better place.

What made 60 Minutes call is in this book.

THE SHIFT

Over the last 325 years, three major asset shifts have occurred in society. Americans have moved from the nation's foundations in the Agrarian Age through the Industrial Age to today's Information Age and with this progress, the asset we value most in business has also evolved.

Beginning in the 1700s, wealth was accrued by owning land and hiring others to tap its many resources, which could mean producing food or husbanding animals for transportation, sustenance, or goods. People aspired to own a piece of property they could build a home on and live off of. So in the Agrarian Age, the land was the major asset.

Then, in the 1800s, came the Industrial Age. Newly invented machines could complete, in a fraction of the time, the work that human beings did by hand. With automation and improved procedures, productivity soared. Thus machinery replaced land as the major asset.

Now, in the 21st century, countries across the world are smack dab in the Information Age. Knowledge and the people who acquired and expanded it now became the major asset. In fact, owning buildings, the land they sit on, and the equipment they house may be more of a hindrance than an advantage in business today.

Companies have been slow to learn that people are now the asset and that they can't treat people—living, breathing assets with thoughts and feelings—the way they used to treat machines or the way landowners used to work the land. With the shift to the Information Age, employees and customers now want, and demand, to be treated as though they matter. They *do* matter, though business has not quite caught on to this new dynamic.

So, what's the bottom line? Every business today has to cultivate a culture that, first, learns what motivates, empowers, and rewards its employees and, second, translates that into positive experiences for its customers. In other words, to thrive in today's Information Age a business must evolve or dissolve.

And even a business that evolves must keep up with what is demanded by society or it will become extinct. It must understand the current wants, needs, and demands of both employees and customers.

Many Americans have been affected by the hardships caused by the collapse of the housing and stock markets, the recession, and the massively high unemployment rate. Think of the events that have occurred: employees have been rocked by the collapse of the housing market and the loss of their savings. They now want to be part of something bigger and better in the Information Age, and they certainly want to be treated like they matter. Customers who were seen as mere dollar signs have been made cynical by corporate bailouts. Today, in the Information Age, they are demanding more choice and a better experience, and they, too, want to be treated as though they matter. Finally, businesses that have been indifferent to employees and customers and have struggled through a banking meltdown now, in the Information Age, also need to evolve—offering more choice and better experiences—in order to be successful.

A business that evolves with the wants, needs, and demands of its employees and customers will survive and thrive. The ones that don't will soon become extinct.

WHY THIS BOOK? WHY NOW?

Occasionally, when I give talks, I ask the audience members to raise a hand if they, personally, have experienced the economic trauma of the last decade or if the life of someone close to them has been negatively affected.

Virtually everyone raises a hand. And when I ask what happened, I hear the same stories again and again.

Some say that they need to get back to work because their retirement vanished with the stock market crash. Others recount that their retirement nest egg was in their house, but now that's "under water," and their equity is gone.

Some tell about an uncle's house that was foreclosed on because of the housing collapse.

Others relate what's happened to friends who lost their jobs in the recession.

The common denominator behind all the pain, strife, and hardship that my audiences and society have experienced is *greed* at the hands of executives, companies, and corporations. That greed hit a lot of hard-working people. And many of them are bitter. Even the few who weren't affected have compassion for the ones who were.

If there's a good aspect to this, it's that we will be less trusting for a long time, as well as more demanding of whom we trust, where we choose to work, and whom we give our money to. It's a sad development, but we are only protecting ourselves. After all, no one wants to be taken in again.

To succeed in the business world today, a company must interact compassionately with the disillusioned men and women, young and old, who are potential customers and employees. This is the moment to take care of people, to tell them you've got their back, and that you're in their corner, not to look at them like walking dollar signs.

Just as in the Great Depression of the 1930s, over the past decade we've all lost a lot of what we worked for—jobs, houses, and retirement savings. For most of us, a big chunk of what we used to have is gone, and we won't be able to forget that any time soon. Those lessons last decades. My grandmother, for instance, learned to reuse aluminum foil and dried paper towels to save money during the Depression, and she maintained the habit for more than 50 years!

The next time you try to treat your employees poorly or "gyp" your customers or even think about raising prices with no reason or benefit, think about your customers and their long memory. Your business with them relies on making an emotional connection, and right now everyone is attuned to even the slightest hint that someone may be taking advantage of them.

THE INFORMATION AGE—TREAT PEOPLE LIKE THEY MATTER

Step back and take a good look at a few of the companies that have been born or are thriving in the Information Age.

Facebook? Sure. People who have been beaten up by the economy want and need to heal; they are interested in connecting with others. That's why social networking companies are taking root: They fill an important need.

Apple? You betcha! With intuitive and innovative products that are easy to use, the company makes its customers feel good and allows them to connect with friends and family more easily.

Zappos? Absolutely. The employees are treated like royalty and they, in turn, have the same appreciation for their customers. That is, I feel, one of the biggest factors underlying our success. In the end we all want to be treated as though we matter.

Amazon? Yep. People have lost a lot of their dough and savings and are working harder than ever trying to stay afloat. With Amazon's low prices and huge selection that can be shipped right to your doorstep, the company saves us time and money, and they treat us right. What's not to love?

And now that we're all empowered with facts at our fingertips, thanks to the Internet, hand-held devices, and smartphones, you cannot afford to regard people as anything less than valued assets, rather than as machines or acres of land. Respect people, show them you understand what they want and need, and demonstrate that you can create a groundswell of improvements in their lives.

EMPLOYEES AND CUSTOMERS HAVE A LOT OF CHOICES

If understanding the importance of treating people like they matter is not enough to convince you that you need to take care of employees and customers, consider how many more opportunities we have today when it comes to where to work and whom we give our money to.

A hundred years ago, your choices were limited. Your job probably was on the farm or close to where you lived. Today, research shows that employees have hundreds, if not thousands, of workplaces to choose from, if they don't mind commuting. They can choose to work remotely or for themselves. Thanks to the Internet, they may not even need a physical store or office to conduct business.

How about the customer? A century ago there were probably just a few stores nearby from which to buy goods. If there was no flour in stock, you waited for the next shipment to come in to make your bread.

Today you can shop virtually anywhere. You're not only not limited to a store close to you, but you can also buy things from around the world with a click of a button on your computer, tablet, or phone.

So if you think you don't have to do a really great job to attract employees or customers—and an even a better job to retain them—you are living in the past.

The Information Age has changed everything.

In the 21st-century marketplace, one misstep and your employee will leave you and your customer will fire you and go somewhere else.

The Information Age has changed everything. The employees and customers of today have a choice and a voice. They are no longer easily ignored, cheap, or disposable. So for companies, remember this: You are no longer the only gal in an Alaskan bar anymore.

And whether you're someone who is unappreciated and underutilized at work or you're an executive who wants to build the best culture for your company, this book will show you the techniques, ideas, and processes you need to get to take your Culture to the Next Level.

PREPARATION IS KEY

Culture is not about "stuff." As I said in the Introduction, Culture first depends on a structure, which always starts with a Vision and a Purpose and includes a Business Model, Unique/WOW Factors, and Values. If those key aspects are chosen properly, your structure will attract the right people, who will create and align the language, beliefs, thoughts, decisions, and actions to it. To put the right Culture together, though, you need to prepare, take your time, and make the right choices, because—I repeat—Culture is not about stuff.

While I was at Zappos, we had a lot of people come and take a tour of our Las Vegas headquarters. There were usually between 50 and 100 folks a day, and they would all come through my office. Most of the visitors I spoke with were amazed at the Culture we had. They could feel the vibe, and they loved it. Looking around, they would see all sorts of different and even crazy things you wouldn't expect in corporate America. For instance, executive row was called "monkey row," because the plastic ivy and vines hanging from the ceiling made you feel like you were in a jungle. Kris in IT placed his desk under a tent so low you had to duck upon entering his space. The one and only Jerry Tidmore was the "Mayor" of Zappos. He had a bullhorn and bowls of peanuts to eat when you came by, and there were shells all over the floor.

Everyone personalized his or her own work space. I even had a throne in my office for all the employees to sit on and experience, just like my visitors did. I wanted to treat the employees like royalty, because they deserved it, and in turn, the employees would treat our customers like royalty, too, which was right in alignment with delivering WOW.

The whole of Zappos was a special place, to say the least.

Many of the visitors said they were going to create a great Culture, too, and some wanted it to be just like Zappos'. The visitors went back to their companies and did a lot of the same crazy things they had seen and liked on their tours. But a funny thing happened. They would e-mail or call me and say that what they did hadn't worked that well. It didn't create the culture and vibe that they had felt while touring Zappos. Why didn't it work? Because they were literally just putting out stuff, and that had nothing to do with the structure that made up their own Culture.

That's one of the reasons I am writing this book: to let people know how, piece by piece, to create or transform their own unique Culture.

I am back home now in the Silicon Valley, where I see the same phenomenon taking place—people using stuff to try to create a culture. At one start-up recently, the leaders painted the walls purple and brought in beanbag chairs and a disco ball to decorate the workspace. There was no Vision, Purpose, or apparent reasoning behind the moves. And the company paid someone to do this! Are you kidding me? The average age of the employees was *over 40*. Was this supposed to attract *younger* employees? They probably could have done a better job by asking the older staff members to sport retro hairdos and wear saggy jeans.

Culture has become a buzzword, and everyone seems to be an expert about how to make a great one. Perhaps it's not that easy to define. The idea of Culture is, I admit, kind of "squooshy." But, believe me, creating a great Culture has nothing to do with simply implementing the crazy schemes of a few successful companies. You have to make sure those changes align with your business and are woven into everything you do, make, and deliver.

CULTURES DON'T SURVIVE ON THEIR OWN

The hippie culture of the late 1960s and early '70s, with its psychedelic art and its rallying cry of "Turn on, tune in, and drop out," was basically a counterculture, but a culture just the same, perhaps the best *ever*. Unfortunately no one created the structure of a business model that would have perpetuated it! Say you want a great culture, but you don't want to put in the time to find out what your employees and customers really want. You risk creating just a house of cards rather than a solid structure, because it's not founded on the crucial building blocks in the architectural blueprints. You need a new battle cry, and it should be: "Get ready, get set, get prepared, and grow."

George Washington may have said it best: "If I had six hours to cut down a cherry tree, I would spend five hours sharpening the ax." And another pretty smart person, Albert Einstein, said the same thing but in a different way: "If I have an hour to solve a problem, I'll use 55 minutes to think and 5 minutes to do something."

When it comes to increasing the chances for success, preparation is key. It works for virtually everything in our lives. Growing up, we learned that proper studying improves our test scores, that following directions contributes to a timely arrival at a destination, and, finally, that preparing the soil will produce a more bountiful garden.

I recently planted some vegetables in my garden. I broke up the dirt, mixed it with enriched potting soil and rooted my seedlings. I had bought too many plants at the nursery, so I placed the leftovers in an area where the soil hadn't been prepared. Four weeks later, I had thriving vegetables in the rich soil. The plants in the unprepared plot were small and wimpy, with leaves riddled with insect holes, and I knew they'd never survive.

Just as you would with a garden, take your time and prepare the blueprint for your company's culture. It may take six months or a year, but the end result will be a bumper crop.

Remember, there are no shortcuts. Take your cue from contractors who meticulously follow plans as they build. In business, the blueprint for the structure includes Vision, Purpose, Business Model, Unique/WOW Factors, and Values. Once these walls, floors, roof, and windows are in place, the interior can be decorated and furnished, and once the people are, inside, they will bring the Culture to life.

When employees know what the company is doing, wants to do, and why it's doing it, then those purple walls or beanbag chairs or crazy schemes will mean something.

The starting point of a great Culture is the Vision of what you are doing. It can and should be a blueprint for what you are going to create, an instrument against which everyone measures their thoughts, decisions, and actions.

- A Vision . . .
- Expresses the focus of *what* your company does or wants to become

OR

- Is what you want to deliver

AND

- Fulfills your employees
- Is in alignment with the times
- Is in alignment with the wants, needs, and demands of the customer

Turn the page to begin constructing a great culture at your place of business by putting these all-important cornerstones in place.

This Is What We Are Doing—Vision

Vision:

The act or power of anticipating that which will or may come to be. Once a Vision is clearly articulated, allow the people to create it.

Before writing your Vision, dream big

Vision is the number one step, for it is *what* you are doing or will be doing.

When thinking about creating a new business, one of the first things you do is visualize what you want your business to become. Having a Vision of what you want to create gives you clarity. By asking you to *visualize* it, I mean imagine two things: How will your business look and feel? What will your business become? Don't be too quick to decide, though. Consider these questions:

Is your Vision big enough?

How wide and how high does your Vision extend?

Does your Vision capture all of the market that is available?

Your Vision has to be bigger than yourself and the company, and it has to be about more than just making money. Employees can get behind a vision of making money for a little while, but if the money isn't spread around, it soon loses its luster.

Creating a Vision for our lives is equally important. Regretfully, some of us have a life Vision that is too short-sighted. Having a big personal Vision forces us to look far in the distance and to set our focus on it. Otherwise, all we see are the obstacles in between.

> *Your Vision has to be bigger than about yourself . . . and more than just making money.*

It is exactly the same with the Vision of your company, team, or organization. Dream and think big.

- State or declare what you want your company to become.
- Match what you want to deliver with what you want to achieve.

This Vision is for you and your team or employees to come up with. Envision the end result and work backward from there. (Keep reading; I'll show you how to get there with concrete examples and how-to information.)

Make your Vision a KISS
(as in "keep it simple, sweetie")

I always advise clients that the Vision of a company needs to be a short, simple, and repeatable slogan that doesn't put boundaries around the company. I've read a huge number of "mission statements" that were two or three paragraphs long, detailing how the company was going to do, what it was doing or make what it was making. But I never could remember even a bit of it five minutes later. Perhaps the sentences were too long or wordy, but most likely—and more importantly—the mission statements had nothing to do with helping me out, whether I was an employee or a customer.

Two or three paragraphs is much too long. Just state *what* you are doing (Vision) and *why* (Purpose). The mission statement (the *how*) will follow with the creative genius of your employees. My feeling is that *you*, as the leader, don't have to state the *how* in a mission statement; let your employees figure out that piece on their own.

KEYS TO CREATING YOUR VISION

When creating your Vision—or updating or transforming the one you have—use the following as a guide:

- Make it current, compelling, inspiring, and motivating.
- Make it a KISS
- Short
- Easy to remember
- Repeatable

- Implement your Vision among your employees, so that everyone knows it and can say it quickly and easily. Over time, try to whittle it down to six words or less. You may not be able to, but the exercise will help your statement be as short, memorable, and repeatable as possible.
- You also want to tie a Purpose with it. (We'll discuss that in depth in the next main section.) But make sure your Vision is short enough to allow folks to remember it and the Purpose, too.

As an advisor and coach, I have had many opportunities to talk to company employees about their company's Vision. Most believe that their company has a Vision; generally, however, employees have been unable to share it with me for one of the following reasons:

- They don't know what it is.
- They don't understand it.
- They are familiar with the Vision but cannot repeat it because it is too long or complicated to remember.
- The Vision is muddled in a long-winded mission statement that makes little sense to them.

Luckily, these challenges can be remedied.

A Vision needs to be simple, repeatable, and well understood by the employees so they can be in alignment with it.

When employees don't know what the company Vision is and only do what they are told, they become disengaged and disconnected, and their daily work becomes uninspiring and non-empowering. Imagine what that does for the business.

If employees cannot repeat the company's Vision with respect and enthusiasm, they're missing a guiding light to direct their thoughts, actions, and decisions.

For example, in a recruiting company I worked with in San Francisco, as we worked to transform the company's culture, we came up with several versions of a Vision statement. But none of them seemed right, especially when we put them to the test to see if they would attract both employees and customers. We knew we were headed in the right direction, but we were having a hard time coming up with a Vision that would stand out in the industry. It's a common challenge. Many of us create a Vision but soon realize it falls short in some regard. If you find yourself in that dilemma, don't give up. I guarantee you will get it right; you just have to keep trying different things out until you do.

So we noodled some more and came up with other iterations of a Vision statement, but none of those came up to snuff either. Finally we hit on the solution, which was this: Sometimes you have to switch it up and come up with a Vision that is *unique in your industry or in what you deliver*, especially if you are in the services business or if you sell a commodity. Since a service or a commodity

Creating the Vision for your company may take several tries before you get it right.

isn't proprietary, you need to be Unique/WOW in your delivery. Think about how your product, service, or knowledge can be delivered differently and what you want your customers to experience. That's what we did with our Vision, and it helped us rise above the rest.

We knew that the recruiting industry was considered somewhat antiquated, with not a lot of regard for service or the customers' experience. Of course, that industry is not alone. Just take a good look at any service business you know of, you'll see that the service part has all but evaporated. So we homed in on this Vision: "To Deliver the Best Service and Experience." That Vision would color every aspect of our business in the future. We started by revamping our training to be top-notch and to deliver the best service and experience; we adhered to best practices in everything we did. Every piece of text our customers saw or read became a visual work of art. After all, if the customer-facing part of our business was not the best experience, it wouldn't be in alignment with our new Vision.

It didn't happen overnight. We were figuring this out as we went along.

Throughout the industry, recruiting methods were basically archaic. The tools everyone used to provide the service to clients and customers were sticks and rocks, so to speak. We decided to develop lasers and rocket launchers, in the form of innovative data, algorithms, and procedures to measure and predict success.

We engaged the entire company in naming our new internal, proprietary technology system, which is revolutionizing the way we do things and is poised to soon revolutionize the industry. We also incubated a start-up—Whitetruffle—outside of the company that helps match candidates and clients and creates an inbound model (as opposed to our going out to find people). After all, how could we deliver the best service and experience if we couldn't expedite our offerings to our clients?

Listen, we all know that in a service company and a service industry you need to deliver service, but that concept has been all but lost. So our particular Vision was to reestablish what we are all about and what we *should* be all about—service and experience—and let that Vision become an overall guide when it comes to specific thoughts, decisions, and actions. With a great Vision, we didn't have to tell our employees what to do, because they knew what needed to be done (and delivered) with the Vision. And that meshes with the three things employees want most: Purpose, Autonomy, and Compensation. The first one, Purpose, you will read about in greater detail later in this book. The third, Compensation, is obvious. But when it comes to the second want, Autonomy, a great Vision ensures that employees are free to do their creative part. They don't need to be told what to do because they know what needs to be done.

When your Vision is "delivering the best service and experience," that's what the employees create and deliver. If it's not the best service and experience, they don't create or deliver it. The Vision helps guide your creativity and delivery and becomes self-managing over time, once it's in your DNA.

It's the Vision; so it's *what* everyone does.

It didn't take long before the recruiting company's Vision attracted employees who didn't want to work at other firms because *we* were doing it differently, and better. They wanted to join a winner. And our customers and clients? They realized that they had better service and a better experience with us, so they kept coming back. Our repeat business started to climb. We grew 300 percent the first year alone, and we haven't stopped since. We made *Inc.*'s list of America's fastest-growing companies two years in a row and climbing, and the firm's two owners made the roster of the Silicon Valley 100.

So is the recruiting company there yet? Has it arrived? No way! The business is just at the beginning of the journey and still has a long way to go. But you know what? The company is definitely going somewhere. And the cool thing is that everyone is on board. Not bad at all for a nine-year-old company whose growth was flat and whose employee turnover was 100 percent. How did the company do it? It transformed and created its unique Culture by implementing the strategies that you are reading about now, in this book, beginning with a foundational Vision statement.

As I said, the company isn't done or even close to reaching its peak. Its new empowering culture is driving its success. Oh, and by the way, the new internal motto is to keep taking it to the Next Level, and that's exactly what they company does, because it is constantly enlarging the biggest room in the house—"The room for Improvement."

So hang in there as you create your Vision. You may not get it on the first attempt. But the reason for doing it will be as clear as glass when you look at some of the great examples later on in this section.

Let your North Star lead
you to greatness

A company Vision, like the North Star, can be a guiding light for employees. It should keep them inspired, motivated, loyal, and pointed in the right direction. A company Vision doesn't need to be about its current products or offerings; it should focus on the opportunities that it can offer or deliver in the future, while keeping customers in mind.

Here's little tale that I hope will paint a picture for you. The company in this story isn't real, but its problem is very real for many organizations I've seen.

Once there was a company that was stuck. It was called the McPherson Aerosol Can Company. It wanted to grow, but since it made only aerosol cans, the firm's leaders knew they could only do so much with their product—change the nozzle, tweak the can shape, or put different liquids inside. McPherson had a hard time differentiating itself from any other company making aerosol cans, and employees couldn't advance because there was virtually no growth. Morale was poor.

What made things worse is that material costs kept going up, and when overseas suppliers came to the market with less expensive aerosol cans, that squeezed profit margins even more. As for employees, not only did no one get a raise, everyone also had to do more work during regular shifts to make up the difference of the company's cost-cutting methods. The future of the company and its employees was looking bleak.

Then something happened. Management was desperate to grow the business, and employees also knew that growth would help them elevate their work lives. So a young employee went to his boss and suggested that the company change its name from McPherson Aerosol Can Company to McPherson Container Corporation. The young man thought that altering the name would open up all sorts of markets. After all, if they could contain things in a highly pressurized aerosol can, they could contain just about anything.

So the name was changed and the new name—McPherson Container Corporation—prompted the company's new Vision: "We Contain All Liquids, Solids, and Gases."

What happened? With its new name and Vision, the company found that it had opened up virtually every market that had to do with a container and was no longer restricted to aerosol cans. From milk cartons, paint cans, and cardboard boxes to plastic bags and shipping containers, there was virtually no end to the products that needed to be contained. The real kicker was that the container industry was stuck in the past, without much reinvention going on. With new designs and enhanced capabilities, the McPherson Container Corporation opened up a bright new future. It could take advantage of all kinds of innovation and improvements.

With changes like these, the company entered a golden field of opportunities. And it began with a change of name and a Vision that became a North Star for all thoughts, decisions, and actions.

What do you think your company can do?

Having your Vision clear not only in your head but also clear in the minds of your team and all your employees will create energy, excitement, and a positive force that will generate amazing results, both in profits and in creating a winning culture.

Here's another simple example: Suppose you owned a limousine company whose Vision was "Taking People from Here to There." What if you switched your Vision to: "Making Every Occasion Special." I bet that Vision would change the way you did things, by aligning your thoughts, decisions, and actions with "Making Every Occasion Special." Just by embracing that new Vision, you would have a different and far more popular and successful business.

How important is it to have a compelling Vision around which your employees focus all their efforts? It's crucial, as you can see in the following fable.

The story of the three masons

In early Babylonia, the king had a Vision: to commission the world's finest and largest stone temple. This was to be his and his people's legacy to the world.

To ensure that the temple was in alignment with the Vision of the king, his highest aide interviewed masons from the three different contractors who were responsible for the project's construction. He asked each one what he did.

The first mason's response was, "I am just stacking brick after brick. I don't know why we are doing this project or what it will become. My boss just told me to stack bricks. It will probably never get done, and I think it is a waste of time." The king's assistant was dumbfounded to hear the first mason's opinion. Didn't everyone know about the king's Vision of the temple?

Talking to mason number two produced a similar result. His response was, "My job is to lay bricks in a straight row. I am not sure what the final project will look like, and I don't know when it is supposed to be completed. I really don't care. My workers and I just do what we are told. The project means nothing to us; it's just a job that puts a roof over our heads and feeds us." Again, the king's assistant was surprised to hear the second mason's comments. Couldn't the mason and his workers see what was being created? It was a temple on the grandest scale. The best marble was ready to be laid on the floors; fine sculptures, carpets, and murals were on hand to decorate this magnificent building. There were clues everywhere about what was going on. The king's assistant was astounded by this mason's inability to understand the Vision of the project and see what the temple would look like.

Asked about his responsibilities, mason number three told the king's assistant, "I am doing my part in creating a masterpiece. I am carefully laying one brick at a time, paying attention to every detail because I am excited to be involved in this project. My efforts will be a part of the greatest stone temple ever built, which will help serve the world and the world's people for many generations to come."

Finally! Someone got it! The third mason understood the king's Vision and was not only inspired to work on the temple but was also honored to be a part of the project. He was doing his finest work. The king's assistant knew that mason number three and his team would do an outstanding job on their part of the project. If only the other masons had the same Vision as the third, this would truly be the grandest temple in the world.

If a company has a Vision to "create the world's finest and largest stone temple," then using inferior products, shoddy workmanship, or uninspired masons will not work.

Think about your own company, your Vision, and your employees. Which of the three masons would you want working in your company? It's obvious you would select mason number three for your team, since that person would share your Vision and enthusiasm.

Now ask yourself, "Which masons are currently working within our company?"

The reality is that you probably have several employees like mason number one, as well as a few who resemble the others. It is frightening to think about how many of them don't have a clue about your company's Vision!

Of course, you want as many of the third kind of mason on your team and in your company as you can get. But you also want them to inspire and convert the others. How do you do that?

Aligning your employees to your Vision will allow them to "own" what they are doing, while increasing their overall happiness and reducing management or eliminating it altogether.

When there is a grand and purposeful Vision, there is less need for supervision or rules.

A great Vision will always attract people

The greater the Vision, the more good people it will attract. A great Vision is something people will like and will want to be part of. It's as simple as that. What is your Vision?

As you can see from the preceding story, it is just as important for your employees to know your Vision as it is for you.

Take a moment and think about each of the following questions:

- Which type of employee do you have in your company? (Mason number one, two, or three?)
- Are your employees in alignment with the Vision of your company?
- Do your employees even know the Vision?
- Do your employees take responsibility for what they do, or do they just do what they are told?
- How do your employees feel about what they are doing?

Knowing the answers to these questions will provide you with a pretty clear indication of the employees on your team.

Having a Vision for your company is a pretty simple concept, but it will help get all employees' hearts beating in the same rhythm, and their efforts moving in the same direction, so it's important to have a Vision.

A great Vision gives everyone in the organization something to focus their thoughts, decisions, and actions on, and once their focus is on the Vision, unlimited possibilities open up. Without that focus, opportunities are missed, and what ends up being created may not be what was intended.

Vision gives employees a focus

A company may say its Vision is to "become the biggest fruit stand in the world," but that doesn't do much for those inside or outside the organization. Unless someone wants to work or shop at the biggest fruit stand in the world—a rather small pool of people, I believe—that Vision will attract neither employees nor customers.

Statements like these express a dream of what you want to happen in the future, and that's okay.

But a Vision has to be geared more toward answering questions like "What you are going to do to get there; what do you want to create or become, or what do you want to deliver? And what do you want your customers to experience?" A Vision should be aimed at attracting employees and customers, and it needs to be aligned with all key aspects of the business aspects.

So, yes, you may have a dream of having the "biggest fruit stand in the world." But by tying it to a Vision of "providing the finest quality fresh organic fruits and vegetables," the statement has the potential to attract employees and customers and can be a litmus test for the thoughts, decisions, and actions of your teams.

In my coaching workshops at Zappos, to better illustrate the power of "focus," I ask attendees, "How many red cars did you see on the way here this morning?"

> *Opportunities to deliver, re-create, and reinvent will follow because of the focus created by the Vision.*

Usually none of those present remember seeing any red cars along the way.

I then ask, "When you go home tonight, please count all the red cars you see, and let me know tomorrow how many you saw."

The next day, the responses generally range from a few to as many as 20 red cars noticed on the way home.

The message is clear. The attendees understood that by having a particular focus in mind they were sharper at seeing that object when it appeared.

This powerful mind-set helped them understand that they needed to focus not on what was wrong with their lives (lest they get more of that) but instead to focus on what they wanted in their lives or what they wanted their lives to be like. If they did that, everything they needed would come into view, just like the red cars.

The power of focusing will keep your "Vision" alive and growing, no matter who works at the fruit stand.

Vision provides something for people to focus upon. Opportunities to deliver, re-create, and reinvent will follow because of the focus created by the Vision.

Put it another way: Vision and the focus it brings will become part of your company's DNA. In turn, the Vision will keep getting stronger and clearer, and you'll be able to determine with certainty what your company will be. And what it will consistently create and deliver.

A great company Vision
energizes everybody

One of my clients put their company's Vision on posters, name plaques, badges, even the home page of its intranet—so everyone could see it, believe it, know it, and live it.

Imagine the positive impact on your company if everyone was working together to fulfill the company's Vision.

Below, I have included the Vision statements from some great, well-known companies. I've also included one from a firm that has been headed downhill for some time; you'll see in that particular case that the Vision is unclear and gives little or no direction. I could point out many other companies with cloudy Visions, but you don't need a lot of examples of what not to do, because we need to focus on the effective ones.

Many companies combine their Vision and Purpose in the same statement. For clarity's sake, however, and to help you create a compelling Vision, I've separated the two elements, highlighting the Vision part of the statements in bold text. (We will be going over each one's complementary Purpose statement in the next main section.)

GOOGLE

> "**To organize the world's information** and make it universally accessible and useful."

Love it. Their Vision is: "To organize the world's information." We can't deny that Google organizes the world's information. Studies show that the vast majority of us who work on computers or use handheld devices rely on Google, and many of us refer to it daily. Google dreamed big—worldwide—when it set its Vision, and the company is rolling along quite smoothly. Did you notice that their Vision doesn't actually say "how" they are going to do it? Telling the *how* would thwart the creativity and invention of employees. That's the very reason that Google doesn't have as its Vision "To sell keywords for Search." That would box them into doing that and that only. Google simply says *what* it is going to do and then lets the employees figure how they are going to do it. Their Vision casts a wide net for opportunities and possibilities to do just that. We'll examine the Purpose—"make it universally accessible and useful"— and the Purposes of the other examples in the next main section.

APPLE

> "To make a contribution to the world by **making tools for the mind** that advance humankind."

Apple is one of the best and most successful companies in the world. And why not? Notice that their Vision—"making tools for the mind"—doesn't mention "products." Tools are useful; products may not be.

Apple's is a great Vision that guides its employees and addresses customers as well or better. Maybe that's why Apple has one of the most devoted and loyal followings a company has ever enjoyed. Again, take note. Apple isn't telling its people *how* to do things or *what* they will be creating; that would limit the opportunities and possibilities. The Vision only states that Apple will be "making tools for the mind"—nothing specific about computers, phones, tablets, or TVs. Again that would limit future opportunities, possibilities, and offerings.

AMAZON

> "**Our vision is to be earth's most customer-centric company;** to build a place where people can come to find and discover anything they might want to buy online."

Amazon's Vision is pretty clear and pretty darn big. It provides a compass for employees and is explicit about what everyone else will experience at "the earth's most customer-centric company." It's no secret why Amazon keeps growing.

Oh, and take a look at the arrow going from A to Z in Amazon's logo. That's a subtle reminder to employees and customers alike that Amazon has everything from A to Z, and even looks like a smile, which is right in alignment with being "the earth's most customer-centric company" to the customer and a gentle reminder for the employees to put a smile in everything they deliver.

ZAPPOS

> "**Delivering happiness** to customers, employees,
> and vendors."

Zappos' current Vision, "Delivering Happiness," is an excellent example of what drives the employees' work and creativity, which in turn positively affects the customers. And it doesn't leave out the folks who make it all happen: The vendors are also included in the Vision. Win–Win–Win.

This is what comes up when you Google Blockbuster's Vision statement:

🚫 "At Blockbuster, diversity means valuing differences. It's
a corporate value that must be continually developed,
embraced and incorporated into the way we do business."

Blockbuster's Vision is pretty foggy. When I read the two sentences, I can't tell what the company is doing or what it wants to do or deliver. Furthermore, I can't figure out quite what it means for the employees or customers, and most likely, neither can they. That's probably a big reason why the company is faltering.

As you can see from these examples, successful companies have a Vision that everyone knows, is inspired by, and implements daily.

And their common thread is that they don't tell people "how" they are going accomplish the Vision. How they do it will change over time, and each company wants its employees to figure it out along the way. Had Apple begun with a mission statement about making the best computers to go up against Microsoft—instead of the Vision they adapted—there would be no iTunes, iPads, or iPhones in our lives.

DOES EVERYONE KNOW YOUR COMPANY'S VISION?

Have you ever watched the television show *Undercover Boss*? It's a perfect example of what happens when employees don't know and can't implement their company's Vision. In this show, CEOs of high-profile companies disguise themselves and spend a week in a variety of "undercover" jobs in their companies. A CEO may be a maintenance worker, an agricultural laborer, truck driver, delivery person, water-damage inspector, computer assistant, waiter, waitress, or theme-park worker. Their fellow employees do not know the CEO's real identity. They just assume the employee is new to the job.

What would you discover if you went "undercover" in your company? What would your employees tell you? And just as important, what would your customers tell you?

The show is an amazing study in human relations, and the experience is an eye-opening exercise for the CEOs. Their week in the trenches shows the executives:

- What it is like to work for the company
- What employees think of the company
- What works and what doesn't

- How they can improve processes and policies
- How loyal the employees are to the company
- Why people matter

The common thread that the CEOs come away with is, "I can't believe that we are so out of touch with our employees, not to mention our customers!" They can't help but notice the results of a lack of Vision, Purpose, procedures, or processes. Once back in their office, their first order of business is usually to focus the culture back toward the employees, rewarding their loyal staff and creating a winning environment for them, as well as for their customers.

One of the biggest rewards is for the company: It now has the long-lasting loyalty of its employees, which will extend to customers as well.

Dump your mission statement

I recently gave some talks at one of the world's largest car rental companies. The company said it wanted to be the best, yet the leaders didn't know what to focus on to truly improve. So I asked everyone what their company's Vision was. They told me they didn't have a Vision. What they did have, though, was a Mission Statement that was posted on the wall, printed on a poster about 4 feet by 6 feet, which they all passed as they entered their workplace. They passed it . . . every day! But no one could even remember two words of it, probably because the mission statement was more than 70 words long.

Can you believe it? A 70-word-long mission statement that's impossible to remember guiding employees' thoughts, decisions, and actions? And without any Vision!

I then asked everyone at the company what separated them from the competition. No one knew. Their guesses ranged from service and selection to price. Oh, boy, was this ever a candidate for a segment on *Undercover Boss*.

So the company didn't have a Vision, but it had a long and confusing mission statement that no one could remember. The employees had no clue what made them different from the competition, and, funny thing, if the employees didn't know, surely the customers didn't know either. Maybe that's why when we rent a car we just choose the place with the lowest price. No one knows why we should choose one particular company over another. The employees don't know; neither do the customers . . . so we go with what is the cheapest or least expensive. There's no better example of why success comes down to having a Vision for your company, the employees knowing it, and everyone making sure it gets created and delivered.

Another reason to dump your mission statement

Here is another example of a mission statement from a company that hasn't evolved. You can see what I mean about the constraints of mission statements.

BLOCKBUSTER:

🚫 "Our corporate mission is to provide our customers with the most convenient access to media entertainment, including movie and game entertainment delivered through multiple distribution channels such as our stores, by mail, vending and kiosks, online and at home. We believe Blockbuster offers customers a value-prices entertainment experience, combining the broad product depth of a specialty retailer with local neighborhood convenience."

As you can see, the statement is way too long. No one would be able repeat it, let alone remember it. Above all, it impedes creativity and reinvention. It demonstrates exactly why you should dump your mission statements and create a Vision and Purpose instead.

Visions need to change now and again

Is your Vision current, or has it faded or been overwhelmed by the need to make a profit? Making a profit is good, but when that becomes the main Vision, you lose something important along the way. If you focus your Vision on the greater good, you'll have more employees all working in the same direction, and profits will flow more easily.

Your Vision needs to be up-to-date and in alignment with the wants, needs, and demands of the employee and customer. This means the Vision should be about giving: what you can do for people.

You can't attract all employees or customers with your Vision, only the ones whose needs and wants you meet, so choose wisely.

What could your Vision be and say that will inspire and motivate your employees? Henry Ford said, "I made the car because I couldn't make a faster horse." His Vision both kept pace with the changing times and changed them in the process. Henry Ford paid his workers a whopping five dollars a day so they could afford to buy the Model Ts they were making! What a brilliant strategy. Employees not only felt like royalty driving their cars, they also provided huge promotional value just by being seen in them. Imagine what Henry would have done with the Internet!

When Amazon came out with e-books, some companies didn't believe these electronic products would catch on. But large brick-and-mortar bookstores have met their demise, and e-books now have a growing market. The Vision embraced by the companies that have closed often ignored the e-book trend. They were stuck "printing the latest up-to-date information for our readers." Alas, the word "print" in their Vision was their mistake and led to their ultimate downfall.

Thanks to the popularity of reading devices like Kindle, sales of e-books have caught up with those of books in print and are surpassing them.

Now other kinds of publishing companies have started to feel the pain, as people have turned to magazines and newspapers online.

When a Vision keeps up with the times and employees truly understand it, they can make better decisions and drive their efforts in the right direction.

Overall, a Vision helps to increase work efficiency. When employees have the company's Vision in mind, their uncertainty fades away because they understand what to do to engage the customer, too.

The following is a great example of an employee who comprehends his company's Vision and is thrilled to be a part of it.

Jason: employee with a Vision

A while back, before I bought an iPhone, I wanted to connect my e-mail to my BlackBerry and spoke to my Verizon representative, Jason, about that. He was very helpful, but after trying several options, we were still unable to sync the two, because I did not have certain information he needed, and he could not access it. He told me exactly what information I had to get, and then Jason did something spectacular: he gave me his direct telephone number! I was surprised, but I was also very impressed with his commitment to helping me solve my problem.

I got the information I needed and called Jason back a few days later. We still had a problem, so he personally went into the Yahoo site and found the information he needed. He connected my e-mail to my BlackBerry, and I was ecstatic!

I also started to understand why he was so helpful to me.

Jason was delighted to be working at Verizon. He told me about phones that were coming out, including a popular model that had sold out in six hours! He shared with me how everyone was "stoked" because Verizon had some "cool stuff" coming out and they were about two years ahead of other companies.

Jason was enthusiastic because he understood Verizon's Vision of staying ahead of the competition and the importance of new products. He felt he was part of something special. And whether he realized it or not, he was part of a "movement" of inspired employees who were helping make the company Vision become a reality.

Letting employees know what you are doing and what you are building allows them to be a part of something. It also helps them to manage the Vision themselves; they can answer many questions, make decisions, and take actions.

The Vision can be a beacon—the North Star and guiding light—for employees as they look for answers and aim for a company's Purpose.

This Is Why We Are Doing It—Purpose

Purpose:

The aim, intention, or reason for which something is done or made. If something is done without Purpose, there is no reason to do it.

Purpose is *why* you do what you do

If the first step in building a Culture is to let people know *what* you are doing, it makes sense that the second step is to let them know *why* you are doing it. That's where Purpose comes in; it is the reason *why* you are doing *what* you are doing.

Forward-thinking companies do more than make money. Their Purpose is to "change the world!" Sam Walton said it best: "If we work together, we'll lower the cost of living for everyone—we'll give the world an opportunity to see what it's like to save and have a better life."

Coca-Cola's purpose is "To refresh the world; to inspire moments of optimism and happiness; to create value and make a difference."

Henry Ford's early purpose for his company was "To democratize the automobile."

EVERYTHING IN NATURE HAS A PURPOSE. WHAT'S YOURS?

Having a Purpose for your company is about *why* your company does what it does. A Purpose gets people excited and puts passion in their effort. It is common for people to want their lives to be connected to something that serves a higher Purpose than they themselves. I believe working for a higher Purpose is in our DNA.

In an emergency, for instance, people may risk their lives in order to save another; they don't think of themselves or their own safety first. They merely react, usually without consciously

Having a Purpose for your company is about why your company does what it does. Why do you do it?

thinking. When asked why they performed some heroic act, most people can't give a clear or distinct answer. They simply say, "I didn't think. I just did it to save . . ." We all have the potential to be heroes; the impulse is inside us all.

Within a company, connecting ourselves to a higher Purpose similarly inspires and motivates people. Employees will identify with a compelling company Purpose, and because of your staff's motivation, your customers will have great experiences and develop their own allegiance to it.

Occasionally, some of us direct our energies toward a lesser Purpose, rewards, for instance. If you tell a group of employees they need to run three miles every morning before they come into work, they probably won't get too excited. But if you tell them that if they complete the run each day, the company will donate money that will feed a family of four for 24 hours, I bet they will exert noticeable energy.

Remember, there is a Purpose for everything, though it may not be readily evident or clearly understood. Some people argue that time spent doing nothing is useless, wasted time. But often, though it's not obvious, we are using that downtime to rest and charge our "batteries."

So when we do anything in our lives, there is always a reason or, more precisely, a Purpose. Otherwise, the act is pointless. Let's take a look at your company's Purpose and how it might be articulated or improved.

Make your Purpose a KISS, too

When thinking about your company, remember, its Purpose needs to be genuine and able to attract others, both employees and customers. Some people have told me that if you create a Purpose that needs to attract employees and customers, it's contrived. But when you stop and think about that, if your Purpose really does attract employees and customers, it's probably the right thing to do, because for the most part, people are attracted to things that are good for them. So, nice job! You are right in line with the wants, needs, and demands or your employees and customers.

Besides manufacturing or sales of whatever your company produces, does it have any other Purpose? Think hard, because there needs to be one; otherwise, you will have a difficult time attracting employees and customers or treating them as though they matter. How do you, your management team, and your employees define *why* you are doing what you do? Could it be . . .

- To produce a profit? That's great. A business has to make a profit to stay in business, but that reason won't rally your employees— let alone your customers—for long, if all your purpose is to line your company's pockets with money.
- To create a way for people to communicate? Even if you are not in the communication business, choosing a higher Purpose can really help your customers communicate with each other. The best way to gain long-term consumers is by word of mouth.
- To create a tool for learning, implementing, creating, or discovering?
- To meet the needs and desires of independent-minded consumers? In today's Information Age, people need to be social, yet they also

want to be self-sufficient. They like to make their own decisions, and the information available at our fingertips has set the stage for this. Buy a TV? We don't want to talk to the salesperson; we want to go online, read the reviews and crowd-source the wisdom, then make up our own mind. We can bypass the middle person and check things out on our own.

- To empower your customers with your product because of your higher Purpose?
- To give your customers something they can rally behind? Will they support your organization by voting with their pocketbooks? Not every business can do what TOMS shoes does. That company's Purpose states: "With every pair you purchase, TOMS will give a pair of new shoes to a child in need. One for One." Wow, that is a real Purpose! Every time customers buy a pair of shoes, they know they're putting a pair on a child in need. What's not to love about that Purpose? Surely it attracts employees and customers. Wouldn't you want to work at, or buy shoes from, a company that helps a child with every sale? TOMS has done something that will "Help make the world a better place," and that's what a great Purpose should do. A rising company, Warby Parker, has a similar philanthropic deal embedded in its Purpose: For every pair of glasses Warby Parker sells, it distributes another pair to a person in need through collaboration with nonprofit VisionSpring.

Now is the time to ask your management team and yourself some tough questions. What *is* the Purpose of your company? Does it help people along the way? Is it making the world a better place? Is it reducing the carbon footprint? Slowing down global warming? Is it putting a smile on someone's face? Are you providing certainty or helping people secure their future? Is it enabling the customer to become more independent and self-sufficient? Is it enriching and empowering your employees' and your customers' lives? Or does your Purpose "use" your employees and customers for your own gain?

A great Purpose will always attract people

People don't get up early because of the money they're paid; they do it when they have a Purpose to fulfill. Purpose changes your employees' attitude from "I have to come to work" to "I want to come to work." People want to be a part of *something that matters*, something that is *bigger than themselves*—causes, for example, or crusades. Men and women will unite around a Purpose, and if it's compelling enough, they'll even donate their free time and money to it.

As I said before, the recruiting industry generally lags behind when it comes to service and experience. So at the recruiting company I worked with, our Vision became "Delivering the Best Service and Experience." For our Purpose we chose "Helping People and Companies Reach Their Full Potential." This Purpose stands out in an industry known for having a less than stellar reputation when it comes to helping folks reach their full potential. I'm not dissing the industry. I've met wonderful people in the recruiting industry, and they are the ones that have told me that helping people reach their full potential is a faded memory.

Once the people and companies we work with understood our Purpose, they appreciated us for keeping their best interest—not ours— in mind. Our Purpose really did attract employees and customers.

Purpose gives our lives meaning. I was recently watching a TV documentary about life in a particular prison. The show pointed out that when prisoners are serving long sentences or life without parole, they intentionally chose to do something that gave meaning to their lives. Some chose to take care of an animal or to help others learn, while others took up a hobby that helped underprivileged groups in some way. The Purpose didn't have to be earthshaking, just something that would give them a reason to wake up each day.

Within a company, a Purpose will help give your employees a reason to show up excited about what they do.

We talked earlier about the three things that employees want most—Purpose, Autonomy, and Compensation. Remember that Purpose is the number one desire for an employee. So, you better make sure your Purpose is a good one.

Without a Purpose, people feel they are wasting their time. In creating a Purpose for your company, think of one that extends beyond your firm's walls. Do you want to serve humanity, save animals, promote ecology, or do something meaningful that will attract people of like mind?

In the spirit of John Lennon's song "Imagine," take time out to do some constructive daydreaming. Imagine if your company, and *every* company, set out to change its Purpose to be really inspiring. Imagine making the world a better place. Imagine going green. Imagine empowering and inspiring your employees and your customers. Imagine helping everyone reach their potential. Imagine doing or making something that benefits us all.

Remember, "*what* you are doing, creating, or delivering" is the Vision, and the Purpose is "*why* you are doing it." If chosen correctly, both answers will attract and retain top-level performers and loyal customers.

People want to be a part of something big, and a great Purpose gives that to them, without your ever having to say a word. It's natural for someone to look at a company and ask:

> "What do they do? Why do they do it? When I find out, I'll see
> if I want to join them."

ATTRACT AND RETAIN EMPLOYEES AND CUSTOMERS WITH YOUR VISION AND PURPOSE

I find it strange that many companies still struggle to consistently articulate *what* they do or *why* they do it. Their company Vision isn't clear, and their Purpose can vary depending on whom you talk to. And yet, these companies still expect employees to flock to them and sign on. Would you really want to sign up for anything (especially a new job) where you had little idea of what you might be doing and no insight as to why? Probably not.

The recruiting company I helped often works with venture capital companies and start-ups to help them staff their firms with top talent. We have had representatives from many different start-up companies come by to give us a presentation in the hope we can excite potential candidates about the opportunities at their company. But here's the crazy part: Many of those companies don't have a Vision or a Purpose, so some of the reps just ramble on and on about what their company is all about. There's no "elevator pitch" that we can understand and repeat to a possible candidate. When we ask, "Does your company do this?" they respond, "Not really." If we follow up with, "Is your company in this space?" They often answer, "Not really." One company rep couldn't articulate anything about what his company did; obviously neither could any of our recruiters. The rep ended his presentation saying, "Just send the candidates to us, and we will tell them what we are all about." But how could we send candidates to a company that couldn't even tell us what it was about, not to mention *what* it did or *why* it did it? It's a shame when companies cannot articulate simply what they are all about. They are shooting themselves in the foot from the get-go. But there is a lesson in it: If you want to attract talented employees, let them know your Vision and Purpose: "This is *what* we do, and this is *why* we do it." It doesn't get much simpler than that!

Let's face it: there are a lot of great companies out there right now, and even though there are more job seekers, the quest to acquire top talent is not easy. The opportunities for good candidates today can be mind-boggling.

Purpose plus Vision don't just equal the power of two: Combined, the effects are exponential for your employees and your customers.

So, if you really want to start attracting the best, it's time to let your potential employees and candidates know what your company is about. Begin by creating and articulating your Vision and Purpose. Those who are interested and who ultimately sign on will do so because they want to accomplish what you are doing and because they feel aligned with the why behind it. As an added bonus, their efforts will all turn in one direction, and over time, the company Culture will even begin to manage itself.

Remember the company that changed its name from McPherson Aerosol Company to McPherson Container Corporation? As I said, from that new name, the leaders created a new Vision: "We Contain All Liquids, Solids and Gases." Well, what if they added a Purpose like "In a Safe and Green Way" or "Helping the World We Live In"? That kind of statement would attract more employees who want to create and design containers that help the world and the environment we live in, opening up even more possibilities and opportunities.

In the next few pages we'll look at examples of compelling Purpose statements from some of the best places to work and the most successful businesses in the world.

A great company Purpose invigorates everybody!

The Purpose of your company, combined with its Vision, will help guide the members of any group, team, or organization to move in the same direction. The two statements act as a channel for the thoughts, actions, decisions, innovation, and creativity that arise in your company.

Let's check out the Purpose part of the Vision statements from the companies we highlighted in the previous main section. Notice how each one's Purpose complements and supplements its Vision.

GOOGLE

"To organize the world's information and **make it universally accessible and useful.**"

Organizing the world's information would serve no purpose if no one could use it or access it. So Google's Purpose is to "make it universally accessible and useful." And accessible and useful it is! If you are like the majority of Americans, you turn to Google on a daily basis to find the information you seek.

APPLE

"**To make a contribution to the world** by making tools for the mind **that advance humankind.**"

"To make a contribution to the world" is a pretty compelling Purpose, and appending the phrase, "that advance humankind" adds a big focus to how Apple makes it "tools." How can the company advance humankind if its tools are difficult to use? It couldn't. So Apple makes its tools intuitive; that is, it designs the kind that need no instruction manual or setup instructions. Yes, that's why people love the tools Apple makes. They are easy to use and readily understood. The company's Purpose is directed by three little words: "that advance humankind."

When you look at Apple's Vision more closely, it's clear that the company knows that Purpose is first on everyone's list, atop Autonomy and Compensation. Apple actually has a Purpose–Vision–Purpose sandwich, where Vision forms the delicious filling between the two slices of Purpose bread (or pita pocket or ciabatta or what have you). Apple starts with a Purpose ("To make a contribution to the world"), then drops in the Vision ("making tools for the mind"), and then culminates with another Purpose ("that advance humankind"). Brilliant!

In fact, Apple took Vision and Purpose to the Next Level by creating the Purpose–Vision–Purpose sandwich. Maybe that's why the company does so well.

AMAZON

"Our vision is to be earth's most customer-centric company; **to build a place where people can come to find and discover anything they might want to buy online.**"

Amazon's Purpose is "to build a place where people can come to find and discover anything they might want to buy online." That undoubtedly helps a lot of folks in the world. It helps me; in the past, if I couldn't find something in a brick-and-mortar store, I went to Amazon, and there it was! The company has been filling a real need. Now when I want something, I go to Amazon first instead of trying to hunt it down somewhere else. I can usually find anything at Amazon, which is exactly in alignment with their Vision and Purpose! Amazon has beome the de-facto first choice.

ZAPPOS

"Delivering happiness to customers, employees, and vendors."

Zappos' great Vision of "Delivering happiness" happens to work equally well for its Purpose, too. Hey, if you are already delivering Happiness, not a lot of other Purposes can top that!

BLOCKBUSTER

🚫 "At Blockbuster, diversity means valuing differences. It's a corporate value that must be continually developed, embraced and incorporated into the way we do business."

If Blockbuster's Vision is foggy, then its Purpose, which elaborates on diversity as a "corporate value that must be continually developed, embraced and incorporated into the way we do business," is an impenetrable cloud. Instead of coming up with this mumbo-jumbo, the company would have done better with a Vision and Purpose that stated: "Delivering entertainment to the world, accessible to all."

Are you implementing your Vision and Purpose effectively?

Like the Vision, your Purpose needs to be well articulated, short, and repeatable. That way it will stay top of everyone's mind, guiding your employees' thoughts, decisions, and actions and resulting in the best experiences for your customers.

And, as we've noted, most successful companies tie their Vision and Purpose together in a way that's easy to read, remember, and repeat.

When employees know, understand, and embrace the Vision and Purpose, they can be their most creative and "own" what they produce. You won't need to tell employees what to do; a compelling and memorable Vision and Purpose let them know what needs to be done—it sets forth the outcome—and releases them to do it in their own ways.

Of course, certain processes will require specific procedures; however, giving employees room to implement the company's Vision and Purpose will diminish their frustration.

A Vision and Purpose also change the dynamic from the tired mode of trying to get people to do something to a refreshing one where they *want* to do it. In the end, less management is needed.

What are you doing to implement your Vision and Purpose?

- How do you inform your employees about your Vision and Purpose?
- How do you remind them?
- How do you reward your employees?
- Who else do you share your vision with? Customers? Vendors? Distributors?

At a staff meeting for one of my clients, I offered an iPad to any employee who could tell me the company's Vision and Purpose right there on the spot. No one had the answer. Not even a few key words. The funny thing is that the Vision and Purpose had been created just six months earlier. What did this reveal about the staff? More importantly, what did this say about their leadership? That they weren't keeping the Vision and Purpose front and center or weaving it into the everyday language of the company.

It is critical that all your employees know the company's Vision and Purpose. Otherwise, how are they going to help create or deliver it?

Here are a couple of ways you can help implement your Vision and Purpose:

- Put the company's Vision and Purpose on everyone's mouse pad.

- Hand out posters. Place them throughout the hallways, in the elevators, around the lunchroom, in the reception area, and on bathroom walls. You want everyone to see the company's Vision and Purpose everywhere! At the recruiting company I work with, we have it written on the wall for everyone to see on a daily basis.

- Highlight it in the company newsletter and on the intranet.

- Organize contests around it.

- Broadcast successes by company employees that are tied to the Vision and Purpose.

- Create a logo or tag line that expresses your Vision and Purpose.

Having the company's Vision and Purpose as an active part of every employee's day is essential to:

- Keeping the Vision and Purpose alive
- Making employees aware of the Vision and Purpose
- Having all ideas, decisions, and actions align with the Vision and Purpose

Look at it this way: The Vision and Purpose serve as the "clothesline" that employees can clip their direction and creativity onto.

A Purpose needs to change now and again

I don't believe that the way we've done business in the past will be accepted in the future. And why should it be? With the speed of innovation and the increase in choices today, no business practice can last forever without evolving.

Ask yourself these questions:

- Have you kept your Purpose current?

- Did your company once have a Purpose that somehow got lost along the way?

- Is your Purpose stuck in the past?

We talked about the fact that Purpose is the number one want, need, and demand of every employee. Here is how we came to that conclusion. Working with the recruiting company has allowed me to compile factual data on exactly what employees want by looking at the reasons they give for wanting to change jobs.

First of all, the company has a database of almost 200,000 engineers. During candidates' interviews, the firm gathers all kinds of information—where they went to school, where they have worked, their specialties, and so on in order to help match the candidates to the companies that would be the best fit. One critical item that is always included has to do with "pain," that is, exactly why these candidates are leaving or have left their company and are looking elsewhere. We have always heard that "employees never leave the company, they leave their boss." That's true. But when we look more closely at the facts, we can see that the core reason has a lot to do with Purpose. Asked why they want to change jobs, candidates frequently respond with these answers:

> "The project I'm working on is not needed, and I know it will be scrapped."

> "I want to be able to make a difference, and currently I'm not."

> "What I do is not valued by anyone, least of all the company."

> "I feel like I'm doing work that is unimportant."

> "I want the ability to have a bigger impact."

> "I don't think the project I am working on matters."

> "I want to make a bigger difference in the world."

> "My design skills are going to waste."

> "No reason to be here."

> "I feel I am wasting my time."

Sure, some of the job seekers want more money, a shorter commute, or just a change for the sake of change. But the highest percentages of folks who leave to take another job do so because of Purpose.

That's right, most candidates leave their company because they have *no compelling reason* to stay. That's because there is *no great Purpose* in their work. So why not make sure your company meets employees' number one want, need, and demand? Sounds pretty simple to me.

There's also a "double-dip" effect of having a great Purpose. We know employees crave acknowledgment and recognition in their jobs, right? Well, acknowledgment and recognition are simply a subset of Purpose. So if you have a great Purpose, the acknowledgment and recognition are built in! Think about TOMS shoes; employees don't need to be "stroked" by management (although it always helps) because they are acknowledged and recognized for putting shoes on a needy child with every sale of the company's shoes. The employees feel great about what they do because of the Purpose that is already in place. Double dip!

IS THE GREATER PURPOSE OF YOUR COMPANY GREAT ENOUGH?

I'm reminded of home-improvement shows on television today. Some of them have the Purpose of renovating a house to bring up the neighborhood. Others are trying to renovate an entire block. Which category are you in?

When you create, transform, or update your Purpose, it is important that your employees, customers, and everyone else know it. Think about the television show that renovates a house in order to enhance the block or the neighborhood. Then imagine a larger scale, with a higher Purpose. You could be changing the city or state—or even set an example for the world!

Yes, a Purpose sometimes needs to be updated, but if you set your sights high enough—on making the world a better place, for example— then usually there's no need for change. Check out your Purpose and see for yourself. If it's tied to helping save the dodo bird or preserving T-Rex, it's probably time to update your Purpose.

Purpose tied to Vision opens new worlds!

You know the story of Christopher Columbus. Initially he had a very clear Vision and Purpose. He wanted to explore the New World, but not everyone was in agreement with what he wanted to do.

Columbus believed the world was round and wanted to prove it. However, everyone else knew the world was flat, kind of like a pizza, and that he would end up sailing over the edge into oblivion. So, to make his Vision a reality, Columbus had to create an inspiring and compelling statement.

His personal Vision—to sail past the edge of the earth—wouldn't convince a crew who were sure they were going to die on this voyage.

So he framed his Vision as, "We will sail where no other ship has been," and he attracted enough sailors to fill three ships.

Now, however, he needed the ships. And the way to get them was to come up with a Purpose that would be tied to that outcome. His reason for sailing where no other ship had sailed, Columbus proclaimed, was to "discover new land and opportunities and find riches beyond our wildest dreams."

That was good enough for the Spanish monarchs Queen Isabella and King Ferdinand. Columbus got his ships.

He went from this:

"We are going to sail past the end of the earth, fall off, and, most likely, die."

To this:

"We will sail where no other ship has been, discover new land and opportunities, and find riches beyond our wildest dreams."

Remember Columbus: Know your Vision and your Purpose, then get your crew and your ships.

It worked for Christopher Columbus; it worked for America; and it has helped generations since.

Your great Vision and Purpose can do the same. Especially if it's fueled by the right Business Model, as we'll see in the next main section.

This Is What Will Fuel Us—Business Model

Business Model:

The plan implemented by a company to generate revenue and make a profit from operations.

Important note

As you move forward to a better understanding of how to create the Culture you want in your company, keep in mind I have purposely written this book in priority, or "building-block," fashion, so you can stack and align each main section with the ones that precede it.

Here's what I mean. We started with the Vision and the Purpose. I devoted the lion's share of information to them because, in any great Culture and company, everyone needs to know *what* and *why* they are doing what they do. Everything that comes after needs to align to those two key aspects of the structure. We then create the Business Model to fuel the Culture and company, and we need to align it with what came before—in this case, the Vision and Purpose.

Just keep building on what you have created earlier. You may need to go back and smooth out a couple of the building blocks, but that will become clear as the process unfolds. Keep on adding to the first five key aspects of the structure—Vision, Purpose, Business Model, Unique/WOW Factors, and Values—and make sure they are all in alignment; then align each new aspect—Culture, Leadership, Human Resources & Human Empowerment, Customer Service, Brand, and Experience & Emotional Connection—to the five key aspects. Be sure that everything you create or transform passes the test of attracting employees and customers.

Choose a Business Model that complements and is aligned with your Vision and Purpose

Can you imagine what would happen if we forgot about or disregarded those who gave us our revenue and those who made what we sell? (Namely, our customers and employees.) Regrettably, many companies do just that.

What is your perfect business model? When did you last update it?

You can either make as much money as you can off customers who will eventually leave you, or you can make a little from the customers who will never abandon you and who will sing your praises to their friends.

Now that you've written compelling Vision and Purpose statements, it's time to turn your sights on creating or updating your Business Model to support them.

Choose the right Business Model

You can't have a great Culture without a Business Model to fuel it and keep it going. In other words, a great Culture needs to be tied to a workable and sound Business Model. Why? As I mentioned in "Preparation is key," the hippie era showed that you could develop a fantastic culture, but without making enough money to carry it into the future, it's not viable. Basically, if a business is not able to sustain its Culture and employees, layoffs will occur. After that, people see the writing on the wall and leave voluntarily. And it's pretty tough to keep up morale and sustain a great Culture when employees are fighting to keep their jobs, are scared, or are leaving. When things go downhill, employees adopt an attitude of being out only for themselves, team spirit suffers, and the same problems are delivered to customers.

I'm not saying that making money should be the primary concern, however; making money should be a priority to keep the business growing and the culture strong, but the first goal would be to align the Business Model with the wants and needs of employees and customers. Treating them like they matter will eventually allow the money to flow—as long as the right Business Model is in place.

WHAT MAKES A GREAT BUSINESS MODEL?

A Business Model should be well defined and focused. This means that the wording is crisp and clear and covers these key areas: Structure, Messaging, Processes, Procedures, and Outcome.

How can you figure out which Business Model would work best for your company? We're going to look at some examples, in order to open up your thinking. You can compare your Business Model, or the one you are creating, with all the opportunities that the Information Age brings, to make sure you have not left out any possibilities or minimized them by having your Business Model stuck in the past. We aren't going to get too detailed—just enough to get your mind percolating with great ideas. If you want more information on Business Models, it's right at your fingertips on the Internet!

Let's start with the "freemium," which Wikipedia defines as "a business model by which a product or service . . . is provided free of charge but a premium is charged for advanced features, functionality or virtual goods." People get to try out a product for free with an option to purchase or upgrade. It's like giving everyone a free sample and allowing them to decide if they want more. What's not to like?

Another popular Business Model is the "platform," in which a company develops a scaffold or stage, as it were, on which individuals and large communities can sell their products.

Amazon and eBay are great examples of platform Business Models, which are in play in a big way today. They capture almost all of what the Information Age has to offer, including cooperation from, and engagement with, employees and customers alike. These models allow employees to be part of something big, which also allows customers to be not only buyers but also sellers, and eventually those sellers can become buyers, too. Theoretically, when it's done correctly, you can double your employee "sellers" and customer "buyers" by creating a platform Business Model.

Some platform or hybrid-platform companies use affiliate and associate programs to let individual contributors create their own businesses while helping the "parent company" grow. The bottom line? A win–win.

Again, I'm not going to get into too many details here about particular Business Models. You should examine what is out there and what is working, because it's often different from the past. I just wanted to mention a few that have taken advantage of the little-known or little-used opportunities and possibilities presented by the Information Age.

Be there (on the World Wide Web) or be square (out of business)

One of the most important things today is to make your company's presence known on the Internet. Even companies with a physical store may not be able to compete in the future without an online presence. Actually, that's why a lot of enterprises have shifted to a bricks-and-clicks Business Model that basically lets them keep their physical store or business but also expand it exponentially by accommodating customers who place orders online.

Not everyone realizes how important this can be. Many people have told me their company has not even come close to expanding its Business Model to capture everything there is to capture. These businesses haven't changed or adopted the Internet as their ally. In fact, some of them haven't even created a website! It's the way of doing business now and in the future, and such companies need to catch up mighty fast or risk falling behind competitors who are speeding along the Information Highway.

Listen to this: I spoke at an annual convention of business owners in the restaurant industry. The audience was made up of the suppliers of 80 percent of the restaurant equipment and goods in America, those who serve hotels, schools, fast-food places, prisons, and so on. Virtually everywhere someone eats, these companies are part of it.

Many of the firms were second-, third-, and even fourth-generation family companies. And the convention-goers let me know that this was a tough business, as far as margins go. Many of the companies had no Internet presence; they were still "old school." And some of these companies that had been around for a very long time were going out of business, because they hadn't caught up with the wants, needs, and demands of their employees and customers in the Information Age. Their Business Models weren't taking advantage of what the Internet could do for them. It was a shame, because I spoke to people who really liked the companies that were faltering. Clearly, however, those companies needed to change with the times.

What are you doing "behind the curtain"?

About 15 years ago, there was a young gentleman who opened up a golf shop in a town close to me. It never seemed busy, so I thought I would stop by and take a look for myself, to see what was up and perhaps to buy something to help him out. I went in and looked around and saw that the shop had mostly high-end golf apparel that seemed expensive and a bit hoity-toity for me. I could see why the store wasn't too busy, and I felt kind of bad for the owner, knowing the pain he must have been going through with a business that was slow.

So I walked up to the owner and asked, "How's business?"

"Fantastic! Couldn't be better," he answered,

Stunned, I looked around. "It sure doesn't look like it," I said.

That's when he responded, "Come with me to the back, behind the curtain."

Well, I followed him to the back of the store, what I saw was unbelievable. There were four people having a blast, talking golf and packing boxes to be shipped out.

"This is where we fulfill the orders we get online, on the Internet," the owner told me. "We make custom golf clubs, re-shaft and re-grip clubs, and sell everything else that has to do with golf. We make ten times more money behind the curtain than we do in the front of our store, which is our testing ground—or our research department, as we like to call it. Right now we are checking out what people like in high-end apparel. That's a huge market, and the margins are great! It helps us find out what people want and let's us know why. Once we figure what people want, we put it up on our online store, and it flies off the shelf!"

The storeowner told me that he hired people who loved golf, so they loved selling and testing the products all day. Though in-store sales were slow, brisk online sales enabled them to keep having fun doing what they loved. A great culture was still there because the business model adapted to changes in retail trends.

To say the least, I was floored and certainly no longer feeling sorry for the storeowner. He was brilliant . . . and that was 15 years ago. He sure got a head start on scaling his business into the Information Age!

How about you?

Is your Business Model a holiday ham?

I have asked many business owners two critical questions over the years:

Why is your Business Model the way it is?

Why are your margins where they are?

Many of them didn't really know where their model came from, but they defended it and rationalized it—and their slim margins—until they ran out of explanations.

It reminds me of a famous story about a holiday ham.

At least once a year, a mother would make her family an old-fashioned ham. She always used the one that came out of a can. You know, those pre-cooked hams packaged in a big tin that opened with a key stuck to the bottom? The mother would take out the ham, make two diagonal slices, each way on the top, put on maraschino cherry halves, stick in whole cloves, and top it with pineapple slices to make it look pretty. And she always cut a bit off both ends before she cooked it.

How are you cooking your ham?

The children could never really figure out why she trimmed the ham like that before she put it in the oven. When they asked her, her answer was, "It was the way my mother used to do it." One day the mother got curious, so she called her mother and asked why *she* cut both off ends of the ham.

The grandmother's answer? Because her roasting pan was too small.

That story reminds me of many Business Models. Everyone keeps doing what was done in the past, and no one really knows why. But the landscape has shifted, and businesses need to change, too.

Most Business Models are old and stuck in the past and continue by default.

Ask yourself:

- Why is your business model the way it is?
- Why are your margins where they are?
- Are you thinking about profits first or working on creating relationships?
- Is your Business Model aligned with the current wants, needs, and demands of your employees and customers?
- Do you find it harder and harder to attract and retain employees and customers?

Just as you need to bring your Vision and Purpose into the Information Age, you need to do the same with your Business Model. Today, choices abound.

Define your market as the foundation for your Business Model

Defining your market is paramount in creating your Business Model. Who are you trying to attract? Don't forget that the Internet and the Information Age have opened up new business opportunities and possibilities for you. Have you rescaled your Business Model to capture all of it?

When defining your market, you may want to take the advice of venture capitalists who, when deciding whether to invest in a certain company, look at the size of the market. One of the most admired of the bunch, Don Valentine, has said, "Great markets make great companies." I've also heard an investor characterize his decision like this: "I don't care what they make. How big is the market?"

In defining your market, you want to identify whom you will be selling your product, service, or knowledge to. Remember, you don't have to be everything to everyone, but you don't want to limit your market either. Consider how some businesses have evolved with the Internet. At the beginning, there were companies that sold online certain items they had to buy, warehouse, and ship. When they examined their Business Model, along with their far-reaching Vision and Purpose, they noticed that they were in business to sell products to everyone, and they didn't have to do it all by themselves. Consequently, companies like eBay and Amazon created a platform business model, which allowed their customers to become their associates and affiliates and to sell their products to the world, along with other vendors. Amazon and eBay kept in line with their Vision and Purpose and transformed their Business Model. They didn't have to physically buy, warehouse, or ship all the products sold by people on their platform, but they got a cut for brokering the transaction. Not only did they have customers, but some of their customers became independent employees.

Creating a "market disrupter" is a good way to bolster your Business Model.

Creating a product, service, or knowledge in a way that your competition hasn't thought of can open up a brand-new market for your company.

Netflix did it when it started to rent DVDs online. Blockbuster and Hollywood Video had bricks-and-mortar stores, and their customers had to physically go to their stores to rent a movie. Netflix allowed customers to rent a DVD at home and have it arrive in a day or so. This created a new market and resulted in the slow demise of the old Business Model and expansive growth for Netflix.

But even market disrupters need to evolve. Netflix movies shipped to your home beat going to a physical store, but now the Internet has become even more convenient than mail. And today companies stream entertainment to their customers, bypassing the mail, which was not too long ago the market disrupter.

What happens to companies
that fail to adapt?

Many companies have failed to evolve with the times and to adapt to the changing wants, demands, and needs of their employees and customers. The following excerpts highlight what happens over time in those cases. They become extinct. It's Darwinian economics.

Langdon Morris, in his 2003 white paper, "Business Model Warfare" wrote about some of the big-name players of the 20th century: "In 1917, *Forbes* magazine created its own list of the largest 100 U.S. companies. By 1987, 61 of those companies no longer existed. Over the seventy-year span, in other words, an average of about one company per year disappeared."

Morris, a Senior Practice Scholar at the University of Pennsylvania's Ackoff Center for Advancement of Systems Approaches, and his team also studied the Fortune 500 from 1955 to 2001 and found that "over this span of 46 years, an average of 30 companies per year left the list."

Similarly, with the S&P list of 500 top companies, "only 74 of the original 500 companies [on the 1947 list] remained in 1997," and "the rate of mortality has been . . . increasing . . . The average life span of an S&P 500 company has steadily decreased from more than 50 years to fewer than 25 years today."

In a Darwinian economic environment, unfit organizations—those that do not adapt to fit new circumstances—do not survive. The message is: EVOLVE OR DISSOLVE!

It's easy to see that the majority of large corporations—even giants that made it through the Depression and World War II—could underperform or fail altogether. They couldn't focus on a Vision, Purpose, and

Business Model that met the wants, needs and demands of their employees and customers. If they had, they would all still be in business.

So, let's look at how the marketplace is evolving and how we need to adapt.

Factor the people of the Information Age into your Business Model

Our society has experienced a shift from the Industrial Age to the Information Age, and business owners and managers need to make sure they have made that shift as well.

People, not machines, are a company's best asset. Yet because of the recent meltdowns in the housing, financial, and job markets, people are disillusioned and wary about being taken advantage of. They need to be cared for and nurtured.

An Rx for your people-oriented Business Model

In deciding on your Business Model, think about this:

Most of the major advancements in humankind have to do with two things:

Reducing Effort
Delivering an Experience

Does your product, service, or knowledge fall into either of those categories? If not, they should.

I used to play a lot of golf with the late ex-CFO of Cisco, John Russell. He was a great guy, and we had a lot of fun, but he was pretty gruff and terse, to put it mildly. Back in the 1990s, when business in the Silicon Valley was really heating up, I thought I'd ask the expert John what the hoopla was all about.

"John, what are all the companies going after? Basically, what's the golden ring?"

He took a long drag on his cigarette, threw it into the grass (as he always did when he hit a shot), blew out a big blue stream of smoke, and said, "D, all the companies want to do is to attach themselves to your home and suck the money out."

Ah, so eloquently said, John, in a way only you could say it. But today I feel that many consumers have woken up to what companies have been doing. Times are changing, and business must catch up to new attitudes, because people aren't putting up with what they have allowed in the past.

Head-in-the-sand business policies

Some companies still maintain a Business Model that embraces these policies:
- Treating employees and customers poorly
- Holding customers hostage
- Having timed contracts that customers need to pay to get out of
- Having lousy return policies for your merchandise
- Telling employees what to do, instead of letting them make their own decisions

I'm not saying you *can't* have these policies in your Business Model; sure, you can keep them up. You can also kick a bowling ball uphill. But be forewarned. Sooner or later, they will be the cause of your decline, because they are totally out of alignment with what employees and customers want today. People in the Information Age are clever about finding companies that treat them like they matter, and they share their feelings. They also broadcast to the world the names of the companies that mistreat them.

People want and deserve to be treated like they matter.

Unfortunately, some companies don't do that because they are trying to keep their costs down. But as we shall see, you don't have to spend much to give your employees respect and appreciation.

RELATIONSHIPS WITH YOUR EMPLOYEES

In your Business Model, you need to engage your employees and treat them like they matter. If you do that correctly, they will return the favor and treat the company the same way. They will become more engaged, creative, and efficient. But if you treat your employees poorly—even if your Business Model meets the wants, needs, and demands of your customers— you're bound to fail. Poorly treated is as poorly treated does. And poorly treated employees treat customers the same way.

RELATIONSHIPS WITH YOUR CUSTOMERS

You've heard the old saying "The customer is always right!" Treating them like they matter is just as important. Talking with them on the phone offers a golden opportunity to build a relationship, as well as create a great experience. Taking that time may seem like a cost, but it is actually an investment. Here's why:

- They called you!
- They have a question, a need, or a desire, and they are looking to you for the solution.
- They will remember a positive experience and think of you the next time they want to make a purchase.

I have spoken with many call-center employees. They tell me that in most cases management considers a phone conversation to have little value. It's seen as an expense, and managers attempt to save money at every step.

- Employees are told to make calls as short as possible.
- They are told to say no, no matter the question or request.

- Some are instructed to hang up whenever they want to.

- They are told to tell the callers that their computers are down.

I was dumbfounded when I heard this. Does saving these few dollars provide long-term value? No. This attitude *costs* the company, making it harder to add or retain customers. Creating a relationship with potentially lifelong customers is one of the most valuable things you can do. Scrimping on service may save a few bucks, but frustrating customers, being of no help, or being curt will always come back to bite you. Poor customer service translates into "short-term gain and long-term pain." As we have learned, Business Models need to generate revenue and make a profit, but they must not forget "who makes it and who buys it."

Poor customer service is like "short-term gain and long-term pain."

Words go viral. What will they say about your company?

Remember, times have changed. In the past, there were fewer choices for employees and consumers as to where to work and whom to buy from. But now, possibilities seem endless, and people have to be factored into the Business Model. Don't think of them as an expense but as an opportunity to secure future success. Above all, we need to serve our employees and customers well!

Service is not the only important factor, however. What people really talk about is their overall experience. In this Information Age, communication takes place at ever-increasing speeds; words go viral on the Internet. Companies can no longer hide behind their poor Business Model.

P. T. Barnum, who is famously credited with saying "There's a sucker born every minute," was able to capitalize on the fact that information traveled very slowly during his time with a traveling circus. In fact, a key part of his Business Model was to constantly move his operation to places where there was "fresh meat."

Businesses of the past could trick or fool people about their products. Snake oil salesmen and medicine shows could dupe unknowing customers and then move on, before news of their false claims and fakery caught up.

Not so today. With Google, Wikipedia, e-mail, text, and other Internet sources, information travels around the globe in seconds, straight to everyone's handheld devices, and information and the truth behind it can be transmitted very easily.

Here's a great example of just how fast news travels these days. Our family decided to go to a movie, and we were discussing which one to see. My wife suggested a film that had been released a week earlier. My daughter, who was 18 at the time, spoke up, "Don't see it; I heard it sucks." A text message from a friend of hers negatively influenced our decision. Word-of-mouth, aided by a high-tech device, had gotten an instant "review" to my daughter. Nothing could have prevented the spread of such information, and no amount of marketing could undo its disastrous effects.

In order to grow, companies rely on their Business Models. Each firm is free to pick a model, but it has to be forthcoming in communicating its choice. The world is more transparent than ever. Current or potential customers and investors all want to know what you're about before they do business with you.

Is your Business Model seasonal?

Last time I checked there were four seasons in business, and they were all earning seasons.

See what your company can do to take the seasonality out of your business. If your product service or knowledge sells more in the winter, sell a related product for the summer months. Or use the Internet; when it's summer here, it's winter somewhere else in the world. Rotate your selling to stay in step with the seasons of the planet. No longer are you confined to your city, state, or even country for that matter. Allow your employees to be creative. I bet they will be more than happy to help your company create a new Business Model or develop related products that would diffuse some of the "seasonality" of your business.

NEVER HOLD YOUR CUSTOMERS HOSTAGE

In today's world, people want to be free to make choices. That's why the old business model of record and book clubs—in which you had to buy a product each month and had no way to opt out once you joined—has all but dried up. Even so, some companies still hold the customer "hostage." Most such businesses are dying out, but a few are still around—and I was one of their victims.

I was suckered a couple of years ago when someone told me about a place to buy books cheap. Since I'm a reader, I thought I'd visit the site and pick up a couple of volumes. The next month I received a book and cassette series about yoga and the pregnant woman. I called the company and let them know that it was a mistake. They told me that it was no mistake, that when I joined, the "fine print" said I would be receiving one book or product a month. If I didn't want it, I could send it back, but I was under contract to buy $200 worth of books over the next two years.

I continued to call the company, but it wouldn't budge. It was my responsibility to read the fine print. The representative said the company got hundreds of calls like mine from people who wanted to opt out, but that wasn't allowed, even though the rep thought it was a poor practice. Not only was the employee apologetic, he thought the contract was not right and felt bad when he had to respond to angry customers. At the end of the day, the employee didn't like the business model and I, the customer, didn't appreciate it either.

Here's another story that's all too common. I recently spoke to a friend who had been with her phone carrier for years, spending upward of $150 a month for the service. She wanted a new iPhone, but her provider didn't carry it. So she paid $200 to end her contract with her existing carrier and signed a contract with the new service and got her iPhone. Although the old company got her $200, it lost out on thousands of future dollars from her—and from the friends, relatives, coworkers, and acquaintances she influenced in recounting her distasteful experience—because it didn't provide its customer with what she wanted.

She went on to tell me that even if her old provider had the phone in the future, she would never go back to them. This is a perfect example of a lose–lose situation. Does your Business Model consist of holding your customer hostage with a contract?

Expand your Business Model to encompass more

Does your Business Model allow for new sectors that can drive your core business, or does it just keep you doing the same old thing? Any business that becomes successful attracts competition, which means the company has to keep ahead of the others by reinventing itself or opening up new aspects of its business.

Cisco Systems is a good example. Every year, it launches new adjacent business units that are designed to ultimately help drive its core business. The parent company fully funds and staffs each new unit and expects it to be a billion-dollar enterprise in five years. If the new division doesn't reach its potential, it's put in the core business, and another business unit is created with the same goal—to be a billion-dollar business in five years.

Cisco's "Telepresence" is one of their successful new business divisions, and it ties right in with Cisco's Vision statement: "The Network is the Platform to Change the Way the World Works, Lives, Plays and Learns." The goal was to create a videoconferencing system that would enable real-time conversations to take place. Up until then, video meetings were mostly delayed and distorted.

Telepresence videoconferencing is on track to meet its financial goals. But what this "adjacent" business also does for the core business at Cisco is to sell more routers to increase the bandwidth that Telepresence demands. It's as if Cisco owned the highway, and it was selling bigger automobiles that increased the demand for them to build more highway lanes.

Remember, opportunities abound in the Information Age. Start new divisions, partnerships, and associate and affiliate programs, or create a platform that invites everyone to come to your company to buy and sell. Expand the services you deliver to your current customers to create new ongoing revenue streams.

The bottom line is this: Customers are looking for a solution to everyday needs. Are you meeting those needs?

Here's a story from my own family. My mother has a dog named Fergie. She planned a cruise and had to find a place that she could trust to care for her dog. She found a veterinarian with a good reputation who had been around for over 40 years and asked if he would board Fergie while she went on her trip. He said he could, but when he showed my mom his kennel, it was worse than a medieval dungeon—not a good place for Fergie.

A friend of my mom told her about another possibility, and there my Mom was greeted by a lovely lady who showed her a beautiful facility. More important was my mother's experience: The kennel owner asked my mother about Fergie and let her know that the dogs played and slept in the same place. She asked for a T-shirt with my mother's scent to put in the dog's bed. She showed my mother the dog food she used and explained that she walked all the dogs twice a day.

Why didn't the veterinarian have such a place? He wasn't keeping up with his customers' demands, even though his profession gave him contacts that could have kept his kennel full. If only he gave the customers what they wanted!

Are there new opportunities aligned with your core business that you are not exploring?

Let's look at a few other examples to jump-start your thinking about how to expand your business.

How can you supplement or specialize your products?

Once you get your Business Model in place and profits are flowing, you can expand your model for additional growth.

Let's say you sell steel by the pound. What if you buy a machine that can produce safety pins with one pound of steel? You could expect to get 100 times more for your steel. What if you turned your steel into razor blades? You probably could sell your steel for 1,000 times more than one pound of steel. And if you could turn your one pound of steel into surgical needles or stents, you could fetch 10,000 times the amount one pound could bring in. Specialization like this is one way to enhance your Business Model. You either sell the material by the pound or you do something with the material to enhance its value.

I have advised many health professionals in the past to specialize their offerings, which helped them stand out from the rest and to become successful. When I moved to Las Vegas to work with Zappos, I met an extremely successful dentist, Dr. Joe Willardsen, who had done exactly what I used to teach other docs to do.

As a dentist, he could have only filled cavities and provided cleaning, but he knew how much a great smile can help someone's self-esteem, so he decided to specialize in cosmetic dentistry. He first invested in himself so that he could be the best cosmetic dentist he could be—as opposed to jumping into cosmetic dentistry without the necessary preparation.

His work has become so well known that he not only works with high-profile celebrities and athletes, he is also the official dentist of the Miss Nevada USA pageant. His work is so sought-after that he opened up a school and lab next to his practice that teaches other dentists the science and art of cosmetic dentistry, and he has professionals flying in from across the country.

Choosing a specialization has provided him with various businesses and a bounty of opportunities and possibilities that he would never have received if he had simply stayed a "regular" dentist.

Some believe that you should list the specific ways that you will offer your products, service, or knowledge, but that will only limit opportunities and possibilities in the future. As technology changes, you will need to keep up with the changes. So just as your Vision should be big enough to allow new opportunities for your company, a well-chosen Business Model will also be complementary to your success and will help fuel it. Don't limit yourself!

Use the up-sell Business Model with extreme care

The up-sell Business Model has been around quite a while and is part of a wide range of industries. How does it work? Customers initially buy one thing and the sales staff tries—and often succeeds—to sell them something additional or more expensive. I'm not knocking the Business Model in its entirety, because it works. But it takes a lot of effort. And frankly, most people don't like it. In the Information Age, there is so much information at everyone's fingertips that customers no longer want or need to be "sold." In fact, they are more equipped to make their own decisions and confident about doing just that.

The up-sell is different from a freemium; with a freemium, you don't have to buy anything up front—the initial purchase is free. You pay only if you want to upgrade or desire more of what's on offer.

One of my favorite examples of a pure up-sell is the experience of buying a new car. I don't know of a single person who likes buying a car. I'm sure you're familiar with the process:

You settle on the price with the salesperson and then are led into an uncomfortable space to do the final paperwork with the "closer." You usually have to wait a bit, and, as your apprehension kicks in, the conversation goes like this:

Closer: "So you want to have the full warranty and guarantee?"

You nervously say, "Yes."

"Good choice," says the closer. "That will be $1,999.00. How about Ever Shield Protection?"

"Uh, I guess."

"How about carpet and glass lifetime warranty?"

"Probably not."

"Do you know how expensive it is to replace your windshield? Do you have kids? Do you think that your kids won't leave the cap off the pen and ruin your seats?"

"OK, I will take the carpet and glass warranty."

On and on the up-sell goes, until you finally cave in to all of the extras. You walk out of the dealership defeated and with a price that's far inflated beyond what you originally negotiated. You may have a new car and like it, but in the process, they "got you," and you don't like *that*.

Ask the tough questions of your business: Are you up-selling your customers to make as much as you can but leaving them feeling taken? Remember, the up-sell Business Model was used in the days when a lot of customers either lived nearby or there wasn't much competition. You could up-sell them because you always had enough new customers, and the old ones didn't have a way to let others know to stay away. You had captive customers, but that's not true anymore, although some big companies still think it is.

Perhaps, as you'll see in the next main section, you should be thinking about other ways that would help you rise above your competition, something that would attract your customers for life and help to secure your company's future.

This Is What Makes Us Stand Out— Unique/WOW Factors

Unique/WOW Factor:

Your Unique/WOW Factors are what make you special, unique, and different from the rest; your WOW Factor is a Unique Factor that elicits a positive emotion. They both allow you to stand out from the others.

What is a Unique/WOW Factor?

For the businesses I have owned, helped, or advised, Unique/WOW Factors have been most important in building an enterprise that stands out from the rest, creates a great experience, and grows by word of mouth. The only difference between the two is that a WOW Factor ups the game by being able to elicit a positive emotion. Think of it as "Unique" and "WOW Unique." I recommend taking great care in creating your business's Unique/WOW Factors, because doing that could be the start of something really big.

Actually, two kinds of Unique/WOW Factors apply to most companies and organizations:

1. **What** you sell (product, service, or knowledge)
2. **How** you sell it (delivery)

Unique/WOW Factors should be part of everything you do in your company, reflected in everything that a customer experiences.

Let me say it again: You should be distinctive both in *what* you do and *how* you do it. And since we've established that Vision is what you do, you should incorporate a Unique/WOW Factor into your Vision, if possible, and articulate it in a way that's easy to remember and repeat and is known by everyone in the company. That way a consistent message goes out to the public highlighting your Unique/WOW Factor.

For an example of how to create Unique/WOW Factor in what you sell, look at what we did at Zappos.

We started out selling shoes. Everyone needs them, and most big retailers sell them. So how could we become unique? To begin with, we stated our Unique/WOW Factor in our Vision: Delivering WOW! After all, who else did that? Then we added other Unique/WOW Factors as well.

A UNIQUE/WOW FACTOR FOR WHAT YOU SELL

Selection

When you go to a large bricks-and-mortar retailer and look for men's Nike shoes, for example, you might see 11 different styles on display. Zappos' website, however, features well over 500 different styles.

A large retailer may stock 100 different brands of shoes, but Zappos carries ten times that—more than 1,000 different brands—and a huge selection within each.

A UNIQUE/WOW FACTOR FOR HOW YOU SELL IT

Free shipping both ways

Many department stores have a sign near their dressing rooms telling customers to take only a limited number of clothing items inside. Can you believe that? They want to sell their wares, but they limit how much you can try on. Here is the rationale: They do it because it cuts down on people stealing. But the truth is that only around 1 percent of the population steals; the stores are just penalizing all the rest.

Zappos allows you to order as many items as you want, try them on at home, and, if you don't like them, send them back for free.

365-day return policy

Some stores give customers a time limit for returns. Some won't give you your money back even if you return a product on time; they offer only store credit. Zappos? You can return anything within a year, and you get your money back. No questions asked.

24/7 friendly customer service

You can call Zappos anytime and get a live person on the phone. (And there's usually no wait time to speak to one.) The representatives are fantastic. They treat you like you matter, and resolve virtually any issue without resorting to a manager because they are there to WOW you! And there's no time limit to how long they can stay on the phone with customers; a call can take as long as it takes.

White boxes

What color are most shipping boxes? Cardboard brown. One way for Zappos to be Unique was to make the box color different. Zappos uses only white boxes, and customers know right away when their Zappos packages arrive. No need to look at the label, you know who sent it and exactly what's inside!

I've spoken to folks at UPS and FedEx, and they love Zappos, too, because the company helps their businesses, and it's super easy for them to identify Zappos boxes in the sea of cardboard they deal with.

In the beginning, Zappos' Vision was to Deliver WOW, but you can see by the list of dazzling features above that the company Vision was woven into many of its processes by creating and emphasizing Unique/WOW Factors.

Think about these examples as you come up with your own Unique/WOW Factors for *what* you sell and *how* you sell it. We'll also go over some others later in this section.

Over time, the public will get to know your company by its Unique/WOW Factor; customers will understand how you differ from other companies, and they will tell other people. Word-of-mouth marketing is powerful indeed. A referral is worth its weight in gold because it comes with the endorsement of those you trust.

Unique/WOW Factors usually will be what you are known for and what your employees and customers say about your company. They could ultimately become your brand.

Frank Lloyd Wright's Unique/WOW Factor in his architecture is captured in his message: "Build of the land and not on the land." His houses were open to nature and flowed with it. He preferred to have most angles in his homes be 120 degrees, which symbolized freedom to him; he was opposed to anything less than 90 degrees, which signified restriction. You can always recognize a Frank Lloyd Wright house because of the factors that make his creations unique, in other words, by *what* he did and *how* he did it.

When choosing and creating your Unique/WOW Factors, ask yourself these two important questions:

What can we do that others don't or can't do?

Will it attract employees who want to create it and customers who want to buy it?

Get those two focuses right, and the future is yours.

Slam dunkin' a doughnut

A friend found this "Social Media Explained" item on the Internet and sent it to me because she knew I was into Unique/WOW Factors and she figured that I'd enjoy the way these social media outlets all had their own twist on a doughnut. I wanted to share this, to show how social media "takes" on a humble pastry can illustrate their Unique/WOW Factors. (They may not be as WOW as they are Unique, but they still set themselves apart from the others.)

Twitter – I am eating a #doughnut.
Facebook – I like doughnuts.
Foursquare – This is where I eat doughnuts.
Instagram – Here is a vintage photo of my doughnut.
YouTube – Here I am eating a doughnut.
LinkedIn – My skills include doughnut eating.
Pinterest – Here is a doughnut recipe.
Last.fm – Now listening to "Doughnuts."
G+ – I'm a Google employee who eats doughnuts.

Virtually all businesses are about selling a product, service, or knowledge. The product, service, or knowledge, however, is only part of the total package.

IT'S NOT ONLY WHAT YOU SELL, IT'S HOW YOU SELL IT

I heard renowned chef Bobby Flay speak about having Unique/WOW Factors this way: "The food may be *what* you sell, but it's only about 20 percent of it. The rest of it is *how* you sell it: the experience, service, staff, training, table setting, décor, etc." They all matter, and they have to be aligned.

Some of us work for a company, and some of us work for ourselves. In either case, we all have the opportunity to create Unique/WOW Factors around what we sell and how we sell it or do what we do. What do you do that others don't or can't? That's what makes you stand out from the rest.

Every great company is unique

Ralph Waldo Emerson viewed every human being as unique; the same can be said of every great company. Without Unique/WOW Factors, you have to sell what you sell by the pound. Why? Because there is nothing special or different about it. There's nothing that makes it distinctive; anyone can make it. When customers know this, you have to go into a price war and struggle for your sales. Without a Unique/WOW Factor, your product is merely a commodity, to be sold by volume or by weight.

What sets your company apart from the rest?

You have to choose Unique/WOW Factors to set you apart; otherwise, you are just one in a mass of competitors.

Let's face it, no one can get excited about a ho-hum experience. No one makes an emotional connection with the "regular" version of anything. A product, service, or information has to be unique to generate a following, and if it's above and beyond everything else around, you can create a movement behind what you do and how you do it.

Unique/WOW Factors are what attract customers and, if chosen properly, will retain customers for life.

In your company, think about what you'd want your family and best friends to experience, and then implement it. Those special features can be your Unique/WOW Factors.

YOU CAN PICK ANYTHING YOU WANT

Unique/WOW Factors can be just about anything you do to stand out from the rest in your industry, or the world, for that matter. Be sure to make your Unique/WOW Factors a positive experience that matches your Vision, Purpose, and Business Model, all of which have to attract employees and customers.

Here's a list of some of the most powerful Unique/WOW Factors that have helped companies expand and prosper. I've placed them in order of their effectiveness in helping a firm grow and succeed.

1. Market disrupter
2. Experience with an Emotional Connection (In the last main section in the book I'll explain this in detail.)
3. Best service and experience
4. Being totally unique
5. Providing service
6. Being different

Feel free to choose more than one Unique/WOW Factor, but once you select them, you must:

- Let your employees and customers know about them.

- Market and promote them.

The best Unique/WOW Factor is one that establishes you as totally different from all the competition. This can apply either to what you make or to how you make or deliver it.

For example, if you own a restaurant . . .

What is the Unique/WOW Factor of your business?
- Service?

- Experience?

- Value?

- Taste?

- Decor?

- Signature dish?

What is the Unique/WOW Factor that describes what you serve?
- Healthy?

- Low calorie?

- Asian? Mexican? French?

- Low cost?

- Gourmet ingredients?

Unique/WOW Factors can involve service, experience, value, quality, exclusivity, limited quantities, low price, high price, interactive activities, or incentives—the list goes on and on. Since everyone wants to be treated as if they matter, service is *always* a Unique/WOW Factor, and it can easily be coupled with others; it can even be a WOW Factor if the service is that phenomenal or special.

When choosing your Unique/WOW Factors, you really want to make them part of your company's DNA. If you choose service, for example, everything you do must align with service as the Unique/WOW Factor, and that starts with delivering great service to your employees. They'll reciprocate by delivering great service to your customers. If service is emphasized within your company, it will be strong enough to reach those outside.

Remember, the experience you give your employees is the experience they pass along to customers. And how an employee is treated is how the employee treats the customer. A badgered staff can't be expected to give exceptional service. It's the same as with pets: If you treat a dog with meanness, the dog becomes mean and reacts in an aggressive, vicious way. Figure out how you want your employees to treat your customers, and then start treating your employees the same way.

You've got to know what sets you apart so you attract both enthusiastic employees and loyal customers.

Double your Unique/WOW Factors and double your success

Whatever you choose as your Unique/WOW Factors, be sure to deliver that uniqueness to your employees first. If, for instance, you choose an enriching experience as one of your Unique/WOW Factors, then you want to give that enriching experience to your employees, too. Start by creating the unique experience at work; it will get into the hearts and minds of your employees, who will deliver that unique enriching experience with energy, vitality, and TLC to the company's customers.

> **Unique/WOW Factors should be something tangible; it's what both the employee and the customer get or experience.**

You can't have blank walls and a dull environment for your employees and expect them to create a unique experience for their customers.

After all, you wouldn't have a recording company and not allow your employees to listen to music.

Here's how John Paul DeJoria, founder of a multimillion-dollar hair products company, put it: "If you can provide the finest quality, you can be in the reorder business and not the selling business." This is a brilliant Business Model, because the outcome happens naturally: The customers who are only interested in bargain prices will exclude themselves from paying for the highest quality. But that's OK; there is enough of a market for those who want only the best.

IT'S TIME TO CHANGE YOUR SALES BUSINESS INTO A REORDER BUSINESS

Everyone in our multigenerational society is now firmly part of an era in which people make their own choices and don't need to be or want to be sold.

No longer is the fast-talking salesperson tolerated. That middle person is going away, unless he or she adds something valuable to the process. Yes, you heard correctly. If you think you can sell something with no Unique/WOW Factor or any added value in the Information Age, think again. A salesperson is a middle person, a means to an end. But today things should be able to sell themselves.

You probably don't use a travel agent anymore.

You probably don't use a stockbroker anymore.

Those two prime examples show how the Information Age has overtaken the middle person, just as cell phones have done away with pay phones. If there is something less expensive and more convenient or efficient to be had, the old means to that end will disappear . . . unless it adds Value. Lots of Value. Or if it's a Unique/WOW Factor.

Extra, extra, tweet all about it!

"THE MIDDLE MAN OR WOMAN IS GOING AWAY"

I repeat: the salesperson in the middle is going away, unless he or she adds lots of Value. Otherwise, the customers will aim for the lowest price.

More than ever before, we trust ourselves to make decisions, thanks to the extensive knowledge on the Internet, now at our beck and call. We no longer need others to advise us. We will make the decision of what to buy. We have become the experts on all things, and if we aren't certain of something, that can be easily fixed with a couple of Google searches.

Nowadays, a product, service, or knowledge needs to sell itself, but to do that, it has to be Unique in some way. Apple understands this very well. It doesn't have salespeople; it has employees who empower the customers. Apple products don't come with instruction manuals. They are intuitive.

When we sell ourselves a product, service, or knowledge, we become part of the reorder business and will keep coming back unless something radically changes for the worse.

Unique/WOW Factors need to evolve

Unique/WOW Factors, over time, don't always stay Unique. Sometimes they become obsolete—yesterday's news, has-beens. I remember growing up with rotary phones: it took a long time to dial a number, but they were much better (I heard) than the phones you had to crank. In the really old days, you had to go through the operator; there was no way to dial directly. Later came push-button phones. Unbelievable! That really decreased the time it took to dial someone's number. Then we got cordless phones. Yippee! No more being stuck to where the phone was plugged in or to tethered the length of the phone cord; "cordless" meant you could walk around and talk wherever you wanted.

The evolution of phones is a prime example of a product being Unique and then not so Unique, then Unique again, then not so Unique, and so on and on.

Here's another good example of a once-superb Unique/WOW Factor that has faded over time. Sears' Craftsman tools were the absolute best that money could buy; once you bought them you had them for life, because if something ever happened to them—say, they broke—Sears would replace them, no questions asked. So you always bought them because you could always take them back if need be.

The Craftsman brand was a huge pull to get men to shop at Sears, and back then, if men went shopping, they took the family with them.

Growing up, I remember everyone having Craftsman tools. Most homeowners did their own repairs around the house, and Craftsmen tools were especially good for working on cars. I used to tune my car, pull engines, change brakes. Virtually everything you could do to a car, my friends and I would do, just like the generation before me. What made Craftsmen tools unique was their quality; so many other tools were made of cheap material, they would break or "strip" quickly. Sears even backed the product up with free replacement if anything broke. To me that was a WOW! When I bought a tool, I knew I would just be buying it once.

But the times changed.

Fewer people use tools nowadays. And by incorporating stronger alloys of steel, other companies are able to match the Craftsman quality, and for a better price. Tools are now so cheap to buy, they have almost become disposable. And since even the less expensive tools don't break down as much anymore, there's really no need to buy expensive tools that you can return.

Moreover, who works on their own cars anymore? I spoke to a group of mostly men whose average age was around 55, and I asked how many of them tune their own cars. One hand went up among the more than 200 people in the audience. I then asked how many of them had worked on cars when they were growing up, and almost every man raised his hand.

Tools have become disposable and no longer need a guarantee. And the once big draw of men bringing their families to Sears has gone away.

What's the lesson? Be proactive and on the lookout to ensure that your Unique/WOW Factors are up-to-date. Because once you realize that your Unique/WOW Factor is no longer working or needed, it may be too late. It didn't happen overnight.

My Unique/WOW Factor

Dr. Charles Ward was the first of many "coaches" who helped me create one of the most successful chiropractic clinics in California and the United States.

When I started the clinic in 1982, I thought patients would be knocking down my door to see me. After all, I had made the National Dean's List, was the youngest (at the time) to graduate from Palmer College of Chiropractic–West, and was the "go-to" guy in the college clinic if any intern needed help.

But the real world was quite different. No one cared about my grades or what I had done in the past; they only wanted to see results. Well, the results did come and good word of mouth followed, but the process was slow as molasses. I was focused and good—even great—at what I did because I lived and breathed my work, but my patients didn't know that. They thought all chiropractors did the same thing, and nothing much distinguished one from another. My bills were mounting. The first year my goal was to make $75,000, and I achieved it, but since I was new in business, I hadn't realized that my overhead would add up to $100,000. Thanks to several personal loans from friends and family, I had enough to stay afloat.

Then I learned that a colleague of mine with an office down the street was doing very well. He did not have my skills; how could he be doing better than me?

So, in 1984 I hired Dr. Ward, to help coach me in my practice, and a short time after, he gave me *the* gold nugget of business success advice. He said: "You have to have a 'Unique Factor' or 'WOW Factor' for your product or service and your business—something that differentiates you from the rest. The WOW Factor means having your customers say 'WOW!'

when they interact with you. Then be sure to let everyone know about it. Some may like what you have and others may not, but you have to pick a Unique/WOW Factor either way. Otherwise, you simply blend in with the rest. You end up with a weak following and even weaker word of mouth."

I was pretty literal back then, so when I chose a WOW Factor, that's what I called it—a WOW Factor.

And I based it on my ongoing training. I was doing research, studying, and going to seminars frequently to be the best practitioner I could be. I invested in myself and my ability to serve others. Then I let my patients, as well as every other employee in the clinic, know that I was learning to "Deliver the Best Care Possible." Everyone knew that at least once a month I was off for the weekend to a postgraduate study course. No messing around ... my patients were going to receive the best care possible. The word started to spread and the clinic began to grow. That was the WOW Factor for *what* I did.

> *Our Unique/WOW Factors are our beacon to attract employees and customers.*

So I picked the WOW Factor of what we were doing and let it be known. But I didn't stop there. I went on to choose a Unique/WOW Factor for *how* we did it. I could have chosen anything, but since the bar of service is so low in the health field, I picked "service and experience" as my business's second Unique/WOW Factor. I was sure to be different if I treated everyone like they mattered and delivered the best service and experience. Again the results were WOW!!! Our motto:

We don't treat the patient; we take care of the person, no matter how small the need.

You see, back in the '80s health care wasn't the best: You often had to wait in old offices with out-of-date décor; it was difficult to get hold of your doctor (there were no cell phones or e-mail); and the overall experience was deplorable. But that was the norm back then. All patients were treated like a captive audience. And if you were sick or in pain, well, take a number. We'd get to you when we got to you.

Here are some examples of *what* we did in my clinic to provide our customers with an extraordinary experience and *how* we did it. (As you go through this list, compare our Unique/WOW Factors to your own recent experiences with a health-care practitioner.)

- We ran on time because we respected our patients' schedules.

- Every patient had my home number and/or the home number of their personal doc within the clinic.

- We had a bright, open reception area, not a waiting room (because that term implied that you would wait), and patients were greeted with a warm handshake or open arms, and then seen by a doc right away.

- We had a billing and insurance department that worked with insurance companies on the patients' behalf, because they deserved it. And patients loved it! (Back then almost every clinic made you bill your own insurance.)

- We had "umbrella service" on rainy days: Someone from the office would personally shelter customers under an umbrella from or to their car.

- We gave patients fresh fruit and other healthy items on a regular basis.

- We had a library with books that patients could read, borrow, and even keep.

- We bought flowers on Mother's Day from a friend who had a flower shop and gave them to everyone. When a man said, "Hey, I don't need a flower, I'm not a mother," we told him to pass it on to his mother, wife, or girlfriend. We would do the same on other holidays, using different colored flowers for different occasions.

Is it any wonder that patients became long-term customers and told their friends, families, coworkers, and everyone else about us? It was a win–win for everyone.

The result of what we did in the clinic was to save lives. Saving lives was our Purpose as we helped to allow each patient's body to work as well as it could and to be as healthy as possible. Our Purpose and Unique/WOW Factors kept us focused and on the right track. The Unique/WOW factors of "Delivering the Best Care Possible" coupled with "The Best Service and Experience" worked extremely well for my clinic. Thank you, Dr. Ward! Your advice has been priceless.

And I'm sure you know about Zappos' success in "delivering WOW"! Unique/WOW Factors can work for your company and enhance your Vision, too, as you "Help Make This World a Better Place."

Your Unique/WOW Factors

So what should your Unique/WOW Factors be? Remember, Unique/WOW Factors apply not only to *what* you do but *how* you do it.

Unique/WOW Factors for what you sell may be in the same category as those for your sales and delivery, or not. Some companies, for example, may choose best quality as the Unique/WOW Factor for what they sell, while for sales they emphasize experience. To get the maximum bang for the buck, though, it's best to incorporate your Unique/WOW Factors into your company's DNA and use it both for what you sell *and* your delivery. That way your branding message is clear.

Here are a handful of great examples.

Bass Pro Shops

This company offers camping items and related outdoor gear, and its quality, selection, and value are not unique; much of the inventory is sold in other stores. However, shoppers go to Bass Pro Shops, because of the way they sell things, for a unique experience. The stores are massive, almost like a theme park. There are fishing ponds and huge glass tanks filled with live fish. There are waterfalls and realistic, bigger-than-life stuffed animals. There even are demonstrations and workshops. Everything in the store is designed for you to have a great experience, and you do! Bass Pro Shops attract outdoor and camping enthusiasts and do quite a business. Just being in the store made me a fan, and I wasn't much of an outdoorsman before I walked in. It truly was a memorable experience, and I'd go back anytime.

The Body Shop

This successful chain of stores has unique bath and beauty products that contain only natural ingredients. The company's principles have been highly publicized and have real significance to many customers. Here is a statement of Body Shop values (Unique/WOW Factors):

We're different because of our values:

1. Sourcing responsibly
2. Reducing our environmental impact
3. Saying no to animal testing
4. Promoting well-being
5. Affecting social change

These are pretty cool rules to live and work by, and I bet a lot of their employees as well as their customers are drawn to them. Collectively these values urge people to join in a movement, and the company donates to worthwhile causes throughout the world, while manufacturing in a green way. How the company sells its products also is unique; it uses the vibrancy and colors of nature to package and highlight its goods.

See's Candies

This company's Unique Factor/WOW for its product is quality without compromise. Maybe that's the reason the business has been around since 1921. Have you ever gotten a bad chocolate from See's Candies? One that was discolored, tasted different, was broken, or less than perfect? Probably not. That's the first thing that a customer wants—*quality and consistency*. At See's, candies are inspected individually as they are put in the sales case or into boxes. Any imperfection and the piece is sent to the back room. It's not even used as a sample. For See's, a perfect chocolate experience is the goal.

The Unique/WOW Factor for *how* they sell the product is also the experience. See's box is beautiful and white, and you get a free sample when you walk in the door—*before you buy*! Most of the employees in the store are sweet ladies, all wearing white uniforms. The company's training program is quite intensive: besides providing excellent service, sales reps must know all the candies and their ingredients by heart!

Wal-Mart

Since Wal-Mart sells products made by other companies, it really doesn't have a Unique/WOW Factor for *what* it sells. Their Unique/WOW Factor has to apply to *how* they sell it, and their choice emphasizes value and low prices. Everyone knows it: Wal-Mart equals value and low prices. When customers want something inexpensive, they can most likely find it at Wal-Mart. Some people have the luxury of not needing to buy things at low cost, but most of us do, and Wal-Mart is the place to go.

What are some of the best Unique/WOW Factors to choose from and deliver through your products, service, knowledge, and business?

Unique/WOW Factors can create connections

Service doesn't mean you get back to someone when you get around to it. At Zappos, the Illustrious Fred (First Employee and our—untitled—president, who, I feel, is the unsung hero of Zappos' success) made it policy for all the buyers at Zappos to return e-mail and correspondence within ten minutes. When the employees made this a habit, things happened for the better: employees didn't wait, vendors didn't wait, and ultimately that set the tone for the customers not having to wait, because that was just the way we did things. It started with Fred and spread from there. (Thank you, Fred, for making that happen!)

Apple's Unique/WOW Factor is creating really cool products. Nearly everything Apple makes is sleek and lighter than the competition's version. The Apple iPhone is just one example; it's loaded with features despite its streamlined shape and size. That's the way Apple makes all its products.

Virgin's Unique/WOW Factor is hipness in every product and service, from its planes and mobile phones to its balloon flights and vacation packages. If you are attracted to something hip, you know where to go!

The Unique/WOW Factor shapes a customer's experience, which ultimately creates or elicits an emotion. If the emotion is strong enough, it turns into that customer's emotional connection with your company.

The Unique/WOW Factor is the starting point, but to me the real boost to this process is the experience and the emotional connection. (You'll read about these in more detail in the last chapter of this book.)

The kind of experience your Unique/WOW Factor creates is key.

- You can have a restaurant with the best food on the planet as your Unique/WOW Factor, but if the silverware is dirty or you have a rude waitperson, your customer's overall experience is not good.
- You can have value as your Unique/WOW Factor, but if the product falls apart, your customer's overall experience is not good.
- You can have hip and cool as your Unique/WOW Factor, but if your product is difficult to use, your customer's overall experience is not good.

When the experience for your customer is not good, it sparks a negative emotion, and if that emotion is strong enough, the emotional connection will be as bad as the experience. They'll remember it forever, and your company will suffer.

The kind of experience your Unique/WOW Factor creates is key.

So whatever you decide your Unique/WOW Factor will be, everything that your customer experiences has to align with it.

If you want to have your Unique/WOW Factor to truly WOW your customers, everything you do, beginning with the way you treat your employees, needs to have that same WOW factor.

A long time ago, in the early 1980s, I had a friend, Mako, whom I lived with in Kapaa Kailua, in Hawaii. Mako used the phrase "buffed out" a lot, meaning to take extra steps to create a fantastic experience for people. The origin of the term comes from polishing your shoes to a high shine so they are buffed out. You can see the result of the extra effort.

A couple of companies I have worked with even started using the phrase "buffed out" or "buff them out" within their company, and it became ingrained in the language and in their DNA.

For example, remember the recruiting company I worked with? Their Vision is to "Deliver the best service and experience" and their Purpose is to "Help people and companies reach their full potential." So when it comes to interacting with people, they create the best service and experience possible.

Here's an example: In the past (before they had the Vision, Purpose, and Unique/WOW Factors), visiting clients or candidates were simply given the office address and an appointment time.

After the company set their Vision, Purpose and Unique/WOW Factors, things changed. An employee would begin by asking out-of-town clients when they would like to meet, for how long, and what they'd like to do while they were visiting. Clients would be picked up at the airport and brought to the office, where they'd be given a tour. An employee would take the visitors out for lunch to go over questions; the recruiting firm's owners might entertain them for dinner, and there might be meetings set up to convey what West Coast business cultures are like.

What are you doing to "buff out" your customer?

One candidate who got this royal treatment (including a photo of her sitting on the throne (the same throne that I'd brought to Zappos) e-mailed a note as soon as she got on the plane for home. The message, in all caps, read: "AWESOME EXPERIENCE."

That was all she needed to say. She had a very positive emotional connection to the recruiting company, and now she won't do business with anyone else.

The end result? She also wants to work for the client.

With the right Unique/WOW Factors complementing and supporting your Vision and Purpose, the only response your employees and customers will have is WOW!

This Is What We Care About— Values

Value:
Worth or usefulness or importance to the possessor.

So what do you truly value? And does anyone know?

OK! Here is where we can tell the world about what we value and who we are. And once we do that, our Values will attract those of like mind and those for whom the Vision and Purpose are important, because our Values are shaped by those things.

We've all heard and read a lot about corporate Values, especially because of some high-profile politicians, CEOs, and even nonprofits that have seemed to be indifferent to them. But, as with all the building blocks of your company's structure, Values, too, must be intricately woven into your company's Culture, if the business is to have a chance at becoming great.

Vision, Purpose, and Values are the main key aspects of your Culture, because the first two are *what* you do and *why* you are doing it, and Values that are aligned with those aspects will attract folks who are going to *create* the Culture or *bring it to life*. Your Business Model and Unique/WOW Factors are the other two key aspects of your company's Culture.

So what do your company and its employees value? Many companies claim to value certain ideas or actions, but if those values aren't reflected in their Culture, it soon becomes obvious those statements are just talk.

Other companies mean well when they articulate their Values, but they use words that are too academic or theoretical and are difficult to interpret and put into practice.

Leaders at one company I visited, for instance, showed me their list of 10 core Values. Yet after reading them, I couldn't quite figure out what all of the points meant. When I asked about one Value in particular, the CEO reread it and said, "In other words, it means . . ." Values should not have to be explained. They should be clearly written, stated, or declared. After all, if your Values aren't understandable, how will they attract employees and how will your employees live by them?

Still other companies commit to laudable Values, such as "responsibility," but they don't realize that responsibility is not a Value, it's a given. Responsibility is what people expect of every organization to begin with.

Make your values unique.

Your company's Values should have a specific meaning within your company and be easy to understand and put into practice. Basically you should be able to live your Values.

For example, you might say you value clear and positive communication. If that's really a company Value, it will be evident in the way coworkers speak among themselves. Listen to what is said and how is it said in your company. Is the language positive? Do your employees say "thank you" a lot? Is the tone uplifting and empowering? Do you recognize and appreciate your employees? Or is the language negative? Do your employees criticize and blame one another? Is the tone condescending? Do your managers chide or humiliate the people on their teams? Whatever language is prevalent, however, you can always transform it. Changes in communication won't fall into place by themselves, but you can create Values that will produce exactly what you want your language and communication to be. And in time the Values you choose will become reality, as long as they are repeated with consistency. Values are also revealed in the traditions within your company. Do you have any traditions? Is there a common practice of giving, serving, and working for the betterment of others? Do you help your employees reach their potential?

How do you "roll?" What about your employees?

VALUES LET PEOPLE KNOW WHAT YOU ARE ABOUT

Just as values are part of one's individual character, they are also part of the character of a company. You can state your personal Values, but you really let others know about your Values by what you do and how you act.

If what you do and how you act are totally the opposite of what you say, people recognize that your Values don't align with your actions—and no one likes a hypocrite.

Many folks have asked me, "How do you come up with your Values? Where do you start?" It's not that difficult, and there is no need to over-think the process, because . . .

Values are what we hold close to us and what we consider important. They are, quite simply, what we Value.

As you and your team create or reassess your company's foundational or core Values, use the observation above to guide your thinking.

Whatever we value, we need to let people know about it. If employees are in alignment with the company's values—that, is, if they commit to them in everyday life (not only at work)—the Culture they create will eventually attract more like-minded employees. Like attracts like. If the employees walk the walk and talk the talk, they will attract more employees like them. And ultimately the Culture will attract loyal customers who appreciate the Values, service, and experience that the employees share.

It must be possible for Values to become part of our daily lives

Whatever we choose as our Values— whether as individuals or as part of a country, religion, team, or company—we must be able to live by them.

For instance, say you value getting things done, and you state that Value as "Always giving 110 percent." Nice try, but "Always giving 110 percent" is an impossible goal. Think about it: Can you imagine *always* giving 110 percent? You would burn out on day one.

Values are different from principles, which are professed rules of action or conduct. Principles are statements of what we do. Values are what we aspire to do and to be, what we hold dear and want to live up to.

Core Values are a blueprint of who we are, what we do, and how we do it

When we are true to our Values, they automatically represent what we do and not merely what we want to do.

By living our Values, we become a reflection of them. That's the reason we must choose our Values carefully, for what is in that blueprint is what we will become.

Values should help guide employees' thoughts, actions, and decisions and, in turn, help the company realize its Vision, Purpose, Business Model, and Unique/WOW Factors.

Many companies hire by their Values and even fire by them. For instance, if your company Values same-day communication but an employee consistently gets back to people after three days, that person is not living up to a Value that has been created. The employee will probably be removed. Most often, though, folks like that remove themselves, because they feel they don't fit in, and, in reality, they don't.

From my 22 years in chiropractic practice in the Silicon Valley (where most of my patients were corporate employees), as the Coach at Zappos, and simply in talking with thousands of people, I have found that there are some common challenges that arise when trying to establish Values. Never fear, there are also easy remedies that can help move the company forward.

Challenge number one

One of the common challenges businesses face when creating Values is that the management declares what the Values are, attempts to put them in place, and gets resistance from the company's employees. If management attempts to sway the employees and still meets with resistance, it often gives up on the process, and then the Values fall by the wayside.

Why does this happen? Because the employees were not part of the process and were expected to live by Values that someone else made up. That would be like me coming into your house and telling you what Values to live by. You wouldn't want me to do that, right? Right. You would probably kick me out! In your house you want to—and should—be part of the decision-making process.

The fix

Allow everyone in the company to take part in the process of creating Values. Over time you can whittle the list down by popular demand, but always make sure the Values are in alignment with the company's Vision and Purpose.

At Zappos, at one point we had over 37 Values; eventually, we pared that to 10 core Values. This is what they are:

Deliver WOW Through Service
Be Passionate and Determined
Embrace and Drive Change
Be Humble
Build a Positive Team and Family Spirit
Do More With Less
Pursue Growth and Learning
Create Fun and a Little Weirdness
Build Open and Honest Relationships with Communication
Be Adventurous, Creative, and Open-Minded

These 10 core Values really make up the company's Book of Life. Employees not only live by them at work, they adhere to them at home, too.

Challenge number two

Management declares, "We have grown too much to get a consensus of what our Values should be."

The fix

You are never too big, nor is it ever too late, to articulate your Values. At Zappos we started creating our Values in 2004, five years after the company was founded, and it took a year to narrow them down. Start the process of choosing your Values, and then let everyone know what you are all about.

Live your Values

Do you value, fun, integrity, relationships, communication, learning, honesty, and respect?

Any one of those Values can help you change the work environment in a positive way and lead to the success of your company.

And the cool part about that is that the employees take the Values home, and their personal life is better, too.

Employees are your company's biggest asset, and the Values you create for your company should empower that biggest asset, not only within your business but also in the employees' personal lives.

We may have many different Values, yet distilling a limited number of core Values is a way of recognizing what we really care about and act on in our day-to-day in lives.

Values must be truly believed and lived.

Getting to the nitty-gritty

Now you've got a feel for what Values are and how they are linked to your company's Vision and Purpose. It's time to get down to the nitty-gritty of brainstorming what you and your team hold dear and selecting the key Values that will guide everyone's thoughts and actions.

Creating your Values is like creating a recipe for a successful life!

To help you begin writing that recipe, consider the following list of "ingredients" that in some way, shape, or form could move your company forward. These principles are in alignment with the needs and wants of the employees and customers of today. The list will help you focus on a starting point for your Values and attract folks who will turn your Vision and Purpose into reality.

- Encourage transparent and open communication. This is what people want today. Remember, we have all been beaten up by the economy, thanks to too many bad decisions by too many corporate leaders. Now we demand transparency and open communication.

- Get things done. People really do like to get things done; they don't want to waste time. Cutting out bureaucracy will help a business stay ahead as long as that Value is in alignment with a great Vision and Purpose.

- Treat people like they matter. Again, we have all—employees as well as customers—been mistreated, so doing the right thing is the right thing to do. People appreciate consideration and will want to join a company that values it.

- Lead people, manage the business. The old way of managing people is dead; if you keep up outdated practices, your company will die too. People need leaders and mentors in their firms to help them reach their full potential. When that happens, the company too will reach its full potential.

- Embrace continual reinvention. This is the only way to survive today. Companies' life spans are getting shorter when they could be getting longer if only employees had the autonomy to create and reinvent more. Values that support a great Vision and Purpose will allow them to do that. You won't believe the results. Incredible!

How many values should your company choose? That's up to you. Some firms have four; some have ten. The numbers can vary. You and your employees should determine what's most appropriate.

What's of greater significance than the number, though, is that each organization needs to have its own unique Values as its foundation.

For example, the Values of firefighters would be much different from those of a nursery school. In each case employees have varying responsibilities as well as different customers whom they serve.

And each group would have a different Vision and Purpose for its organization. The firefighters' Vision might be to "Save Lives," whereas the nursery school staff might embrace a Vision of "Nurturing Lives." The values of each would be built around those respective Visions and Purposes. (In both cases, the Visions actually have Purposes tied to them, because "saving" and "nurturing" are not only *what* they do but also imply *why* they do it.)

So what could a great Value be if you are saving lives?

Teamwork, caring, courage, community, to mention just a few. The list includes how firefighters work when they rescue folks, and also the people they're committed to. (My sincere thank-you to all firefighters and police officers; our lives and safety depend on you.)

And what would be some Values if you were Nurturing Lives?

Patience, love, kindness, compassion, among others. Can you imagine if your child was enrolled in a nursery school where all the employees lived these Values? You would love it and would pass the word to every parent you knew!

It's up to your company to determine who should choose your core Values. What I have seen work best is to get all employees' input on the Values that their company should adopt. If everyone needs to live by them, it only makes sense to elicit everyone's thoughts.

Unfortunately, I have seen executives, CEOs, and management dictate the company's Values and then present them to the staff. This is usually met with resistance.

The unfortunate results of no Values

- A disconnect between employees and management
- The inability to stay on schedule or meet deadlines
- Poor treatment of employees and customers
- Poor management skills coupled with poor leadership
- Employees' lack of empowerment to help the company

Above all else, please remember this: The Values you choose should allow your employees to reach their own potential, personally as well as professionally.

When the employees are empowered in their own lives, they will raise the company with them.

Values should be beneficial; they are meant to unite, inspire, and motivate. They should be transferrable to the next generation through the corporate DNA, while remaining flexible enough to be relevant to needs of future employees and customers.

Walking the walk and talking the talk

Are the leaders in your company a good reflection of your core Values? Do they live and breathe your Values on an everyday basis? Whether they are or are not, people can see it.

Think about it. Do you know someone who says he is honest but lies and cheats? Have friends boasted that they are living green, but they drive gas-guzzling SUVs, buy cases of bottled water, and never recycle the plastic containers? Do you know people who say they are all about giving but hang on to money like skinflints? Their Values are livable, but they are not living them.

When we see people say one thing but do another, we tend to discount their statements; we know they are being hypocritical. We probably would like and trust them more if they were honest about who they really are.

I've met some people who are tight with their money but don't try to hide it. It's OK, because they are open and honest about their spending. They're totally transparent. And we all know people who are always miserable and would complain if they won the lottery. That's okay too. We like them anyway because they don't profess to be something they're not. They just love to complain.

Remember Enron? The company's stated core Values were *Respect, Communication, Excellence*, and *Integrity*. But there was a huge disconnect between the company's words and its

Core Values have everything to do with your Culture and ultimately affect how you do business and how your business does.

actions. The firm had all sorts of objects that proclaimed their core Values. Their Vision and Values were even written on paperweights. However, Enron's values were not at all aligned with its Culture. The company had a brutally tough Culture that was implemented when a new CEO came on board. If the Values had articulated the new attitude, at least people would have known what the firm was all about.

Part of Enron's Culture was a process that involved a Performance Review Committee. Employees called it "Rank and Yank." Every year people were rated from 1 to 5 by their peers, but the leaders decided in advance that 10 percent of employees had to be rated as 5s and 15 percent had to be terminated. So one's job security was voted on by everyone else. That made self-interest job number one, and doing anything to keep your position, even if it meant taking another employee down, was standard procedure.

Enron should have put up signs that said "Be Nervous" and "Be Scared" to help send the message.

The company's business involved trading energy and energy services, and Enron was aggressive in its deals, which resulted in heavy gains but ultimately also heavy losses, and that was the company's downfall.

Enron actually had a cutthroat Culture, but you wouldn't know it by reading its stated Values.

Some great people joined Enron because of the success it initially enjoyed, along with the Values the company professed. But these employees found that the Values weren't what they thought. They had been deceived, and once inside, it was sink or swim for them.

If a trader could show better results and make a bigger commission by stepping on a coworker, he did it. As one trader put it, he would actually try to "crush the throat" of a fellow employee. They all looked after themselves and no one else, which meshed with the company's real Culture and Values—being aggressive, tough, and cutthroat.

They would have been living their Values if the list had mentioned Greed, Cheating, and Lies. That might have attracted some aggressive traders to join the fray, but probably not a lot of clients or investors would have wanted to work with them.

Enron cooked the books to hide its losses, which for a long time fooled many people. In the end, though, not living their Values is what did them in. If only they had lived their stated Values, they would have been fine. At a time when many people feel that corporate executives are less than trustworthy, people want to know what they are really all about.

How far from Enron is Oprah Winfrey, whose name alone evokes a positive response? Oprah's consistent message—from her interviews and television talk show to the articles in her namesake magazine—is all about self-empowerment and living up to one's potential. And she lives that Value in her widespread philanthropic endeavors, such as funding a girls' school in Africa.

If we are living up to the core Values that we declare, people perceive us as a shining light.

There are so many wonderful Values that can empower our employees and that can, in turn, strengthen our companies. We just need to go through the process and choose, with the input of the entire team, what we want our core Values to be. Keep the following in mind:

- You should value relationships, which allow your employees the freedom to leave and the opportunity to come back. After all, that's what you want for true friends.

- In a great Culture, the unwritten Value is always to do what's best for the individual.

- Values should positively attract employees and others, including customers.

- Values allow your Culture to manage itself.

Many people have asked me, "Once we create our Values, how do we make sure that they stay our Values and are adopted and lived by our employees?" The answer? Once you attract those who value what your company Values, you don't have to worry about making sure they will uphold those Values. That's a main reason why they joined your team. It's just the way things go: those who are in alignment with your Values will join the company and will attract others like themselves. Those who aren't in alignment with your Values will leave. In that way, the Culture begins to manage itself.

This Is What Is and What Could Be—Culture

Culture:

The totality of socially transmitted behavior patterns, arts, beliefs, institutions, and all other products of human work and thought. The sum total of ways of living built up by a group of human beings and transmitted from one generation to another.

Culture is the life of any company or group

Culture is the living, breathing, thinking, and creative sum of all the beings in a particular group. It is their collective thoughts—their beliefs and ways of thinking— actions, and decisions. When such a group of people acts as one, anything is possible.

Conversely, if a Culture is fractured in any way, the whole is less than the sum of its parts. If everyone isn't going in the same direction, a Culture will be weak and unhealthy.

For a Culture to be great, the people in it must have direction or a reason to exist. Remember our key aspects—Vision, Purpose, Business Model, Unique/WOW Factors, and Values? These all support the structure of the Culture, and then the people who join in bring the great Culture to life.

As you get your Culture "right," make it part of your company's DNA.

This is the United States of America, "Land of the Free"! It's the melting pot where everyone can enjoy a Culture of freedom, liberty, and choice. For generations millions of people have sacrificed to move here from other countries. Emigrants in search of liberty and freedom have even died attempting to come to the United States. As Americans, we strive to be free, and the world knows it.

Americans' yearning for opportunity is every bit as strong as that desire for freedom. Most of those immigrants have been motivated to work hard for a better life, something not possible in their native lands.

Freedom was the reason the United States of America came into existence. In July 1776 the authors of the Declaration of Independence wrote of the inalienable human rights of "life, liberty and the pursuit of happiness."

Wow, what a Vision! As for the Purpose of "the pursuit of happiness," well, that couldn't be much more attractive if it had a chocolate bar tied to it. Way to go, America! This country was, and still is, the place to be.

In September 1787, the authors of the U.S. Constitution wrote in the Preamble about securing "the Blessings of Liberty" for posterity. The Constitution creates the perfect blueprint for a great and long-lasting Culture, one in which we're all free and empowered. Like the blueprint for a company, it has all the key building blocks that we have been talking about in this book: it defines what America is about and attracts those who want to live in its Culture. In the Constitution we have

- Vision

- Purpose

- Business Model

- Unique/WOW Factor

- Values

all rolled into one.

It took time to create the Declaration and the Constitution, which provide the structure of the Culture of the United States; creating and developing your Culture also should be given as much time as is necessary.

Just as the Declaration of Independence served as a blueprint for American Culture—attracting employees (citizens) and companies (businesses) for more than four centuries—your business, too, can have a Culture that will stand the test of time.

This nation's founding documents have been successful in attracting folks because the statements in them meet the wants, needs, and demands of people here and around the globe. You, too, can create a Culture that attracts others and grows in the same fashion.

MAKE SOME MAGIC HAPPEN

What is the Culture at your workplace? Is it a place of freedom and opportunity? Do the employees enjoy liberty and the pursuit of happiness? Is there a clear path to advancement? Can employees elevate themselves and the lives around them by adding more value to what they do? Why would they want to work in your company if it doesn't even provide the same freedoms they enjoy in everyday life?

I was in a meeting with Mike Abbott, then Vice President of engineering for Twitter, and we were talking about what really attracts employees and inspires them. It's not just money. The acknowledgment and recognition of others are crucial. Equally important is one's own passion, which is fueled by the freedom to create and solve critical problems. Mike put it eloquently: "People don't get up at 4:00 a.m. because they are making a million dollars a year. They do it because they are excited and passionate about what they are doing. Money isn't everything. They want to create, they want to frame a problem or have it framed, and then have the freedom, liberty, and opportunity to figure it out and create the solution. They want to have a Purpose."

That is the biggest element missing in many large companies today. Most employees don't have the freedom to create a solution. The Culture—because of the leadership, its bureaucracy, or the Business Model—puts the kibosh on the creative impulse. Even companies that are touted as "Great Places to Work" in reality may not always be great for individual employees. I read an article that put a well-known company near the top of the list, but some of its employees let me know personally that it was not the best place for them. They worked 70 to 80 hours a week, and even though they were rewarded with perks and salaries, they still felt stifled. There was a mismatch between the employees' Values and those of the corporate Culture.

When you give a group of people a great Vision and Purpose and stop telling them what to do, then magic can happen. Employees already know what needs to be done; you've told them what that is with your Vision and Purpose.

Again, the Vision is *what* you are doing, and the Purpose is *why* you are doing it. The magic is what employees will create and deliver.

From my observations, it makes the most sense to create a Culture that is empowering, engaging, and creative for all employees. Their attitudes and behaviors will soon be mirrored by the customers.

If executives really got the importance of a great Culture and its positive effects, everyone would be happy to come to work. Instead, statistics prove that more than 90 percent of America's workforce would rather be employed somewhere else. Businesses pay the price for this in high rates of employee and customer turnover. If only management would wake up and smell the coffee.

If your Culture is aligned with the key aspects of your business, and it's engaging and empowering, your employees will soar on their own. Your Culture can either kill great ideas or give them flight. It's the same with reinvention, creativity, and teamwork. So the question to ask yourself is: "Does our Culture provide freedom, opportunity, and the liberty to create and reinvent?"

A SEPARATE VISION AND PURPOSE FOR CULTURE?

Before we go any further, I want to make this point very clear. On occasion I have been asked a question like this: "OK, Doc, I understand that you need to have a Vision and Purpose for the company, but what should the Vision and Purpose be for the Culture?"

Good question, and the answer is always the same: The Vision and Purpose for your company is the same for the Culture. It's the Culture that will bring the Vision and Purpose to life with language, beliefs, thoughts, decisions, and actions that are in alignment to it.

Say we had a social media company that had as its Vision and Purpose "Unifying the People and Countries of the World; Helping to Create Unity and Peace." The Vision and Purpose of the Culture would not be "Making Pancakes, Because They Taste Good." No, the Vision and Purpose of the Culture would be the same for the Culture as it is for the company. It's just that the Culture needs the structure of the Vision and Purpose to form language, beliefs, thoughts, decisions, and actions around.

In short, use the same Vision and Purpose for your Culture as you do for your company.

A great corporate Culture is an asset to any business

Culture, if created, implemented and sustained correctly, not only helps attract employees and customers and strengthens their allegiance to the business but it also helps with the bottom line

I was watching CNBC the other night and saw a show a titled "The Costco Craze: Inside the Warehouse Giant" that included an interview in which the company's cofounder and soon-to-be-retired CEO Jim Sinegal said, "Culture isn't the most important thing. It's the only thing!"

Actions do speak louder than words

There are all sorts of national cultures. The culture of a country comprises shared values, traditions, etiquette, holidays, food, and a language that helps produce common ways of thinking.

In my clinic, I treated many people who worked in the Silicon Valley. Some of the patients came from Japan and spent a year or two at Toshiba, Sony, or other high-tech companies. Right before they returned to Japan, they always brought me a beautifully wrapped gift. The first time I received such a present, I was floored. I had received gifts now and then, but these were different.

The patients returning to Japan never missed fulfilling this custom—not once. Whether they had an appointment or not near the time of their departure, they dropped by to thank me and give me a gift. It didn't take me long to understand that this was part of their culture. That realization prompted me to think about Culture and how it can propel a company to become the best.

Aligning all parts of your Culture with where you want your company to go is a must. The people within the Culture are the ones "rowing the boat." If you want to go anywhere, you've got to take care of who and what will get you there.

For example, all sports teams have a Culture that's reflected in positive language, a focus on winning, and on being the best that athletes can be. Everything within the Culture needs to be aligned to those things—thoughts, beliefs, traditions, work ethic, even food. The more successful and victorious a team is, the higher its ticket and sales revenues. Losing teams need to change their Culture, since doing what they have always done and believing what they've always believed in is responsible for their losses.

The most successful sports groups in the world have always stressed the Culture of teamwork. No surprise there—a team cannot win unless all the individuals work as one.

Creating ways of thinking that align with the Vision, Purpose, and Values of your company will get your employees working in a single direction. Eventually the Culture of your company will be your identity or your brand. No matter what you sell, your Culture will be evident by the way people interact in and with your company.

A great corporate Culture is an asset to any business. Studies have revealed that companies with a Culture aligned with the key aspects of its business and its goals routinely outperform their competitors at 200 percent or even more.

This book isn't about having a Culture just like the one created at Zappos. It's not a "how-to" book for you to replicate what was created by some other team. Culture is an identity that only the members of each individual organization create because it's what they themselves think, value, and do. It's not some recipe we can duplicate.

So be true to yourself as you build your Culture. Nothing great is ever achieved trying to imitate something or someone else. We need to create our own culture by figuring out what, together, we do, think, and care about.

You already have a Culture in your company

Many of the men and women who took a tour of Zappos and stopped by my office told me, "I want to create a culture in my company!" My respectful response was always, "You already have one."

Any group, from a country to a company or team, has a Culture. A Culture consists of a group's commonalities, which can be fractious or uniting. We all are part of various Cultures—national, regional, local, familial—yet it's the Culture at work that has the most impact on employees and customers.

The Culture in your company may support individualism or teamwork. It may breed contempt by the way employees are treated. It may be a lean culture or it may be described as a "fat cat" attitude. Whatever characterizes people's thoughts, beliefs, feelings, and actions *is* your Culture.

Ask yourself, does your Culture unite your employees toward your common Vision and Purpose? Do the individuals in your company even know its Vision and Purpose?

We all want to be part of something that is bigger than ourselves, something that makes a difference. That's the reason the Culture needs to be tied to a great Vision and Purpose.

A story from one of my former patients really brings this home. He was a webmaster at a company whose employees were so smug about their past success that they barely did any work at all.

When the webmaster first hired on, he was seated in a room with two other employees. The first time someone from a different department came in and asked the team when they could finish a project, the new webmaster spoke up. "I can have that back to you in two days," he said.

Afterward his teammates were furious. "Never do that again!" they told him. From now on he was always to say, "Between two and three weeks." Why? That way they wouldn't have to work so much.

The sad thing was that that kind of behavior spread throughout the company until it became their Culture, and the business—which once had over 10,000 employees—went bankrupt.

You can have people on your team, but success comes only when you have those people on your side.

I can remember when my daughter, Victoria, was in her mid-teens. If I asked her to stand up, she would, but I knew that inside she was stubbornly still sitting down. At that age, most of us don't want to do what our parents want. Thank goodness, it's usually only a phase.

We must understand that an employee or team may go through the motions of doing what they are told, but if they aren't engaged, the results can be disastrous.

Is this going on in your company? What does it say about the Culture that's taken over? Would you like to create a different Culture? Read on.

What makes a great Culture, or makes a Culture great?

As I mentioned before, many of the people who toured Zappos were so wowed by its Culture they wanted to take it back to their own companies. They associated Zappos' Culture with its 10 core Values. And that's a great start, but core Values are only a fraction of what really makes up a Culture.

Some executives told me that though they came up with their own core Values, nothing seemed to change in their companies. Others attempted to make their work environment more fun, but productivity and accountability went downhill.

The success of a great Culture is predictable, but you have to understand what really goes into creating one.

KEYS TO A GREAT CULTURE

The word "culture" comes from the Latin root *cultura*, which means to cultivate or till the land. Plant the right seeds, and through proper care and nurturing they will flourish, and you'll be able to harvest the produce you want. Those seeds are like the structure of your company. As employees join, they "tend" the Culture, keeping it alive, and the business grows.

Vision and Purpose

As we saw earlier in the book, Vision and Purpose are the key aspects supporting any Culture. You may have heard management say that you need to "be on the bus or off the bus," meaning that everyone on the team should be going in the same direction, together. But where is your bus going? And why? Does everyone know the destination? And is there a good reason to aim for it?

Common language

All cultures have a common language.

But over time, without constant work to keep the language aligned with the company's Vision, Purpose, and Values, that language will be diluted. Often a language originates with the voice of the founder or the CEO. As more people join the firm, it's easy for that founding voice to become a distant memory.

How do you keep your common language alive? Leaders need to be constantly aware of what is said and how it's said in the company. Is the language positive? Is it negative? Is it condescending? Is it uplifting and empowering? Are the leaders keeping your common language intact?

At Zappos I put motivational posters around the inside of the building, which helped create a "can-do" mind-set. You can be equally effective, albeit with a totally different outcome, if you put up signs around your workplace that read, "My boss is a tyrant," "My manager doesn't care about me," "The company treats me poorly." Those messages don't have to be true, but if you are surrounded by them each and every day, the negativity will soon become the common language of your employees.

So what guides the language inside your company? Are the Vision, Purpose, and Values clearly stated and easy to discern?

Or are there signs that tell employee what they need to do on a daily basis or rules they need to follow? That sure puts a damper on an individual's quest for empowerment and autonomy.

I once visited a rapidly growing company whose COO wanted to raise his workers' productivity. He told me that some employees thought they were better salespersons than they really were, so he rigged up a huge monitor that displayed the metrics of the top-producing employees in blue and those of the bottom-producing workers in bright red. He thought the device would bring up production. But all it did was lower the esteem and morale of the worst performers, while the top employees spent time commiserating with their coworkers. It would have been easier and less expensive if the COO had just made the laggards wear dunce caps. That probably would have gotten the same negative results. By the way, the COO isn't there anymore.

Beliefs

All great Cultures have beliefs. That's what makes the Culture what it is. What characterizes your Culture? Does it rely on employees who can figure things out and take the company to the Next Level? Does it empower and serve employees and customers? Or does it stress profits at any cost, even if that kills the goose that lays the golden egg?

Many of a company's beliefs are revealed in its overall Values. Earlier I mentioned Jim Sinegal of Costco, who said, "Culture is the only thing." Well, he helped create a company Culture *that believed in keeping prices down*. While other places might offer a $5 hot dog, then imagine how to squeeze 25 cents more out of their customers merely to make more profit, Costco does everything it can to keep its hot dog *and* a soda at $1.50. To maintain that price, Costco changed its condiments and brought in soda machines instead of selling soda in cans. If it's what the Culture *believes in*, it's what the culture *does*—no compromise.

What does your Culture believe about its employees and customers? You answer that question by what your company does.

Attitude

The attitude of a Culture is the "vibe" you get from everyone. Is it positive or negative? Do the employees of your company think the Culture is great or are they wondering if it would be better to work somewhere else?

In my clinic we hired people who were great at what they did, but our basic premise was to "hire for attitude and train for aptitude."

At Zappos, hiring for culture fit was about 50 percent of our process, and it ensured that everyone who entered the Culture could fit in and have fun. As a matter of fact, one of the core values at Zappos was "create fun and a little weirdness." It didn't mean that we had people who weren't experts in what they did. We just helped them work as a team and see the big picture of the Culture. Then we let them create.

If we only hired people who were rock stars in what they did but couldn't get along with anyone else, we would have had individual rock-star contributions but dismal teamwork, communication, collaboration, and relationships.

So what is the vibe in your company? Are employees tense? Looking over their shoulders and covering their backs? If so, something is horribly wrong. What's missing? Is there a Vision and Purpose? Is the Business Model shaky? Does everyone stand behind your Values and understand your Unique/WOW Factors? Hopefully this book will help you understand what's shaping the negative attitude, and you'll be able to implement the right fix.

Work ethic

Work ethic is about *how members of the Culture work*. Do they spend long hours alone in their cubicles, or do they take time to communicate with their coworkers and create better relationships? Do they arrive early in the morning? Stay late at night? Whatever the work ethic of your company, it should balance growth and creativity. "Working people to the bone" means we end up working with nothing but bones. The point by now is familiar: We need to treat people like they matter.

Countries differ in their work habits, such as hours and vacations. For instance, in Spain, workers take siesta around midday, then go back to work and stay later into the evening than Americans do. Europeans usually enjoy six weeks' vacation, while Asian workers get two weeks off for the Chinese New Year. Around the globe, cultures are defined by what they do, as well as why and how they do it.

The average U.S. employee spends approximately nine hours a day at work and commuting to the workplace, five days a week (a majority of waking hours on those days). Isn't there some way company leaders could thank their employees for spending so much of their time at work?

One of the companies I am involved with has a task-oriented culture that seems to be aligned with the wants and needs of today's employees; as a result, the business is doing rather well. The whole team gets together every Monday and maps out the work to be done for the week. Then they all go their separate ways to meet the goals. The company attracts employees who like to work alone without distractions. I talked to one worker to get his feedback on the Culture. "I like it," he said, "because I go to sleep working on my laptop and wake up with it. Most of the time, if I have to get ready and travel to work, it's a disruption."

I don't think that the corporate world consciously intends to work its employees too hard. It's just that many executives are still linked to the old style of management and the mind-set of the Industrial Age, when machines were the biggest asset and labor was dispensable.

Five minutes or more

I've been to Mexico on many vacations. When I took my wife to a resort there for the first time, she asked the housekeeper for two more towels to take to the pool. The woman said, "Yes." "When?" my wife asked. The answer was, "Five minutes or more." What does that mean? My wife wondered. Soon? An hour later? Longer?

Over the course of our stay, we asked for extras several times, and each time we would get the same patient answer, "Five minutes or more." We joked about it, and after a while we knew that whenever we asked for something, it would be some time until we saw it. Eventually that attitude helped us take our time, too—after all, we were on holiday!

The housekeeper really helped us understand the culture of being in Mexico on vacation. She taught us to relax. And that's what we were there for. We just forgot.

I'm sure some employers would like to get all the productivity they could from their employees, but that can only happen over the short term. Running a full court press, as in basketball, can only be done in short spurts. Loosening the reins a little may actually produce the effect you want. When employees are treated like they matter, they are much happier, and happy employees don't quit nearly as often as unhappy ones.

There are huge costs tied to the loss of continuity and the efforts of rehiring. Companies estimate the cost of replacing an employee at between 50 to 200 percent of the person's salary, more for someone in a management position.

On the flip side, if your Culture does emphasize hard work, let that be known as well, so that everyone understands what's in store. A Culture with a hard work ethic will appeal to its own kind of employee. As the saying goes, there is a lid for every pot.

Building relationships with coworkers

The work ethic at Zappos included elements that may sound counter-intuitive. For instance, we were all urged to spend up to 20 percent of our workweek outside the office with our coworkers. Executives from other companies often cringed when they heard that. But we felt that we would be more efficient at our jobs if we built better relationships with one another. The same premise governed the lunchroom, where the food and drinks were free. That allowed us to "break bread" with each other and know our coworkers better. It went along with one of the company's core Values, which was to "build open and honest relationships with communication." Our frequent company "happy hours" also encouraged all employees to let their guard down and just socialize.

Most people need and want good relationships with coworkers. What is your company doing to foster that?

There's a well-known Silicon Valley company that doesn't care about creating an environment that encourages employees to stay for a long time. Quite the contrary, the firm hires "gunslingers" for development in the belief that anyone who excels in the technical field will stay only for a short time anyway. It's assumed those employees have an entrepreneurial mind-set and will want to move on and create something new. Why cater to them when they will leave soon enough anyway? That attitude is part of this company's Culture, and there is nothing wrong with it. It works for them and for certain employees. You just want to be open and honest about that kind of Culture up front.

To create and maintain a great Culture, focus on the keys: Vision and Purpose, of course, then a common language, beliefs, attitude, work ethic, and building relationships with coworkers. At times you might need to focus more on one element than another. But that's to be expected. Creating a culture is an organic process because you're working with the living, breathing employees who bring it to life.

Transform your Culture for the better

Culture either has to come from the top or be green-lighted by leaders; otherwise, it will not be sustainable. People always follow the actions of those in charge. Even in a family (which is a mini-culture), kids are a reflection of their parents. You can see this in the way members of a family stand or move; it's not genetic, it's imitative. They say teams mirror management. What that means is that if you are in management and behave one way yet expect those on your team to act differently, you are in for a rude awakening. They will follow your lead. That's how teams mirror management.

But here is something interesting.

Not every CEO has a personality that matches the company's desired Culture. If your CEO is quiet, cranky or curt, for instance, it might not matter as far as the overall Culture is concerned. All that CEO has to do is approve, green-light, and encourage a Culture with a more relaxed and positive vibe.

I have seen super Cultures with a less than likable CEO at the helm; that was not the individual's style, but the person could check off on the Vision, Purpose, and Values that drove the desired Culture and could hire those who would keep it moving in the right direction.

Just because some CEOs can't play the piano doesn't mean they don't enjoy listening to piano concertos, and they still may want to bring in the best pianist in the business!

So take it easy if your CEO isn't naturally happy or empowering; leaders like that can still be great leaders and recognize the benefits of a great Culture. You just have to let them know what is needed.

One reason companies are hesitant to transform their corporate Culture is that they think it will be too expensive. Yes, you might have to spend something to make changes, but don't discount the benefits, like more repeat customers. That can result in great savings, since the cost of acquiring *new* customers is always on the rise. Keeping the customers you have is like compounding interest with the added accrual of new customers brought in by word of mouth.

Another reason companies don't try to transform their Culture is that they think they would never be able to completely turn things around. Just as Rome wasn't built in a day, so, too, this is a step-by-step process. A Culture doesn't pop up instantly. You need to make a plan and follow it.

There are intrinsic challenges with combining different cultures, which may happen when companies merge or when a new CEO steps in. Cultures "clash" because they reflect differing ways of doing things, different Values, and contrasting Visions or Purposes. The challenge is to understand those differences and come up with a clearly articulated plan for how both cultures can work together.

Any Culture can be combined with another. The process just takes a little time, some give-and-take, and an understanding of what the combined Vision and Purpose should be. Remember, if you can combine the Vision and Purpose and make the results compelling, you will attract and retain those who want to create it.

No one likes change except a wet baby, but everyone needs it.

Cultures change. Over time everything evolves. Look around: Change takes place every day; the world doesn't stay the same.

Actually, we all love change in what our five senses experience. The more variation in what we hear, see, touch, taste, and smell the better, especially because all we have to do is sit back and take things in.

What people *don't like* is change in their routines. Because then we actually have to pay attention and create new ways of doing things, until the new routine becomes automatic.

There is no need to resist a cultural change if it is warranted by the group or dictated by evolution or law. We simply need to reframe the issue so that the benefits are clear.

Implementing the Culture that is right for your company is up to you. But there will be much less resistance to change when the Culture has been created by the people who have to live it.

WHEN DO YOU NEED TO CHANGE?

Creating a great Culture from the beginning is ideal, yet when companies are small and focused on building a business, they don't always take time to articulate what they want. Instead, the Culture usually takes its cues from the founder or CEO. That may be OK for a while; a start-up team is usually small enough for communication, direction, and focus to remain clear. As the team grows, though, things tend to get a little loose. It's best to describe the Culture in a blueprint for future generations as soon as possible. Doing that becomes urgent when a company starts to lose its relationships, communication, common language, and traditions.

Some say it's inevitable for companies to lose focus on their Culture as they grow; they claim that size precludes a winning mind-set. I don't believe that's true. The Culture may not have been what it once was or what anyone wants. But you can certainly redirect it. If a culture gets watered down or changes, it's because preserving it wasn't a priority.

You don't have to accept that your company Culture can't be transformed. But you may need to hire someone who can help shift the focus and then make sure everyone knows about the new direction. Is someone doing that for your company?

Who is driving your Culture? Who is championing it?

If you are trying to transform your Culture, asking your employees what they want is crucial for them to "buy in." Creating your Culture should be fun and can involve everyone in the company! After all, you have the chance to create an environment in which they'll love to participate. Granted, once you decide on the Culture you want, some employees may leave, but that's inevitable; soon the Culture will be managing itself, attracting those who are in alignment with it and turning away those who aren't. Sometimes you have to pull weeds to make the grass grow.

Great cultures bring people together and keep them together. When you tie your Culture to your Vision, Purpose, and Values and line up the group's thinking and actions, you produce a powerful sense of unity, and anything can be accomplished.

You may find there's some give-and-take until the new Culture is created, but the results will be well worth the work.

LAW OF ATTRACTION

Remember this: When you create or transform your Culture, you'll attract the folks who want to embrace your Vision and Purpose, and you'll find many of your customers will do the same. It's impossible to come up with one culture for everyone. Don't worry. Define what you stand for and what you want to attract, and recognize that you can't be all things to all people. Only a milquetoast Culture fits that description, and in the end it actually attracts no one at all.

If you define your Culture as hip and cool, hip and cool people will flock to you. And if you want a Culture that is all about delivering service, start with the employees who were drawn to that goal. Make flags that say, "We're Here to Serve" and put them around the company to keep the Culture on track and the service vibe strong.

A company's Culture should attract like-minded employees. It may not draw from the largest pool, but then, we all don't necessarily like the same things. Some love big cities, others prefer to live deep in the woods. Figure out the kind of Culture you want to have, understand the opportunities and challenges that are inherent, then go for it!

Every Culture must be transparent

Once you choose your Culture, make sure everyone knows what it's about. If you want to attract employees who crave a fast-paced culture like New York City, and that's not apparent, you may inadvertently hire someone who prefers a laid-back atmosphere. That person wouldn't be happy at work. It's important to be clear about your Culture up front.

For example, does your company consider e-mailing on weekends a standard practice, or do you, in the interest of balance, e-mail only if absolutely necessary?

One of my best buddies starts work every Sunday about noon and keeps at it until late in the evening. He might get an occasional e-mail from his boss on a Sunday afternoon, letting him know that he has to prepare a 50-slide PowerPoint presentation by Monday morning. No big deal. My friend knew from the beginning what he was signing up for. He matches his employer's Culture. Not everyone will.

At the opposite end of the spectrum there's O'Neill Clothing USA, part of the La Jolla Group, a multi-brand action sports–licensing organization, whose CEO is Toby Bost. The LJG headquarters has a skate park, a basketball court, and a full gym. Not to mention a retail store. You can bring your dog and your surfboard to work; two surfboard closets are outfitted with racks for your gear. It makes sense: If surf apparel is what the company sells, having employees live the surf lifestyle has long-term benefits. Nice work, Toby! Way to go, O'Neill!

Some people like a demanding Culture, others don't. It's better to be transparent about yours; otherwise you'll end up with one of two things— a disgruntled employee who stays or a disgruntled employee who leaves. Either way, you lose.

Why not create a Culture where your employees can soar?

Some technology companies—and even "regular" companies with a technology team—have set up specific periods where their developers and engineers can simply create. During these 24-hour "hack-a-thons," employees can come up with anything they want. You just have to set up a great environment, slide them some good food, and let them go. I have seen some pretty cool products emerge from hack-a-thons, which are now in wide use.

The creative results—some label them genius ideas—didn't come from anybody being told what to do. Employees had total freedom to create. Management simply removed the leash, so to speak, and let them run.

Often when we are told what to do, we'll do it, but the task seems like a chore and we are always checking the clock. When we are free to create something on our own, though, time flies by. We "own" what we do and will work harder to make it better than if someone had told us to do this or that. So why not allow your employees to do the same? All you have to do is change the dynamic from "having to do something" to "wanting to do something."

We live in a great country where we have all the opportunities we could wish for. In general, we can make more money by adding value to what we do or applying ourselves more to whatever we choose. So why would we ever opt to spend most of our waking lives somewhere that offers less freedom than we have in the outside world? Most folks don't want to work in an environment where there is no chance of advancement, where the atmosphere is dictatorial and demeaning, or where all the talk is negative. People want to join a Culture that couples significance with success. That's why money is number three on employees' lists of needs, wants, and demands, behind Purpose and Autonomy.

We must understand that employees' lives go beyond their work. If you create a "can-do" mind-set in your employees, they will make a positive contribution in their personal lives and in the company as well.

CARE ABOUT EMPLOYEES, AND EMPLOYEES WILL CARE ABOUT THE COMPANY

If we want loyal customers who come back to us, we need to put effort into encouraging loyalty in our employees. I have seen firsthand that when you treat people like they matter, they will shine in every way. Treat them poorly, and the company will go downhill.

Often visitors to Zappos told me that their company didn't treat employees well, and that produced poor results in every aspect of their business. Uncaring employees won't show up on time, they'll call in sick, and the turnover rate will spike. Even worse, those employees will never innovate or take their jobs to the Next Level in any way, shape, or fashion.

Maybe that's why the average life span of S&P companies has shrunk from 50 years to 25. Corporate America has been using people and valuing money, when it should value people and use money. Many in management know that their employees are unappreciated, and they compensate them with money. But you don't have to spend a lot to create a great Culture. Caring for employees doesn't cost that much; consider it a modest investment in time. Even some of the "Best Companies to Work For" don't truly understand this fact. They may say they have a great Culture and treat employees well, but not every worker agrees.

These companies have perks like on-site massage, valet service, free food, nap pods, and such, but their staff members still may be unhappy. Why? Because though they enjoy amenities, they miss personal attention. It's like rich parents giving their kids everything money can buy but none of their time. Those kids don't want stuff, they want to be treated like they matter . . . but unfortunately their parents are just too busy for them.

Spending a lot of money won't guarantee a great Culture. But what about the investment of time? Time is money, right? Well, how much time does it take to greet employees or get to know them? Believe me, those gestures are well worth the few minutes they take.

Employee attrition is the leading symptom of a poor Culture.

Do your employees want to "hug" your company and its Culture? People who like their Culture aren't eager to leave because their workday is enjoyable and empowering. I'll ask again, is your culture in alignment with the Vision, Purpose, and Values of your company? If so, your employee attrition could be as low as 5 percent.

The not-so-surprising effect of a low employee turnover rate is that you will also have a low customer turnover rate. Think about the simplicity of that statement.

If employees are leaving, it's a sign your Culture is not that strong and neither are your Vision, Purpose, and Values. Or you are saying one thing and doing another. Many of the companies that have contacted me, big and small, have a turnover rate of more than 20 percent. At least the fact that they're asking for help shows that they're committed to getting better.

A good test for executives is to ask themselves this question: would my children be treated as if they mattered if they worked in my company? Would they be taken care of and be properly led so that they reached their potential? Basically, would I want my children to work in my company?

If the answer to these questions is no, then it's time to change the Culture, because even though your kids may not be working at your company, someone else's are.

Communication is essential

Communication is key to maintaining a great Culture. We'll go into that more in the next section on Leadership. But communicating a common language, beliefs, traditions, and celebrations is what keeps a Culture thriving. And conversely, lack of communication leads to what's sometimes called the death spiral of Culture.

I have found that the biggest challenge in a growing company is a disconnect in communication. The once unifying voices of the CEO, founder, and executive team become more muted and are misinterpreted by employees the farther away they are from the source. This leads to poor communication and strained relationships, and ultimately the Culture morphs into one where no one really knows what's happening or what they are supposed to do.

I've also noticed that as the organization grows to around 50 people, or when the company starts to be organized into different teams or divisions, communication weakens even more. That will continue unless processes and procedures are put in place to keep communication tight.

What can you do? To keep communication, relationships, and the Culture at their best, I advise all my clients to have the executives get together for an "alignment," "collaboration," or "unity" meeting once a week for an hour. The main purpose is to create a common language, provide cohesion, and form relationships around the Vision, Purpose, and Values first and then around the Business Model and Unique/WOW Factors.

During the meeting everyone takes a turn, tells how their team or division is doing, and where they may need help. It's also a good time to highlight how each team or division is weaving or "baking in" the five building blocks of the Culture into their processes and procedures or into the product, service, or knowledge that they are creating or delivering.

By doing this, the executives keep a timely finger on the pulse of what matters for the business and the employees. And everyone stays in the loop and remains directed toward success. The bonus is that there is never anything to "fix," because if things are addressed once a week, nothing has a chance to get "broken."

Often executives have told me that there are too many meetings, and they don't want to attend weekly gatherings. But I can say with certainty that when no meetings take place, communication within the company starts to break down, and no one knows what is going on or where they fit in. Employees gossip or make up stories, as they do in any group. That's just human nature. Relationships break apart, and unity disintegrates.

As teams and divisions become isolated and do their own thing without weaving in the Vision and Purpose, the Culture and company head downhill.

The sad irony, when there is a disconnect in communication, is that executives actually end up having more meetings trying to put out fires caused by employees who don't know what's happening or who are not getting along.

DO YOU RESPOND QUICKLY OR SLOWLY?

How does your company communicate . . .

- Internally, with employees?

- Externally, with customers?

Responding quickly is paramount to getting things done, and it lets others know that you care about them.

Wherever I go, I emphasize that e-mail or phone calls need to be returned the same workday or within 24 hours. Why? Because when someone needs your help, a delay in responding hinders what they're doing and tells them they don't matter to you.

Sometimes I receive replies to questions weeks after my inquiries. That gives me a clear view of what that company thinks of me, how that company is doing, and how poorly it keeps up with the times.

How can you tolerate delayed communication these days? This is the Information Age! If you are too busy for me, well, then, I will simply go somewhere else.

One start-up business, whose managers included some of the most seasoned and well-respected executives around, asked me to help with its image. The firm needed to add staff, but the hiring process was so tough most prospective candidates didn't make the cut. And after going through long interviews, unsuccessful job seekers let it be known that they considered the company "a bunch of arrogant [expletive]" (in the words of the executives). Executives wanted to change that image, because it wasn't a true image and it was not helping them meet their goals.

I began by checking on the hiring process, which wasn't that easy. It was tough just to get the information I wanted; I tried several times to ask questions of one employee who clearly felt no urgency to respond to me. And as I looked into procedures more, I could see that communication was sparse, to say the least. No one got back to candidates in a timely fashion. There was no phone call to let them know that they didn't make the cut, just a brief, impersonal e-mail. The company certainly didn't treat prospective employees like they mattered.

So what was the fix? The first step was to communicate with job seekers as the process unfolded. Those who weren't hired had to be let down with respect and dignity. That way their experience would still be positive, they could move forward with their job search, and they'd be less likely to bad-mouth the company. Image saved!

Culture is tied together by communication, and it comprises what is thought, written, and said. A Culture of like minds draws particular people to a business and keeps them there. The old saying "birds of a feather flock together" couldn't be more correct.

Some employees are attracted to a Culture immediately or perhaps they warm to it over time. Others like the Culture they grew up with and seek out something similar. Still others rebel against a Culture and go looking for another.

Have you got the company Culture of your dreams?

Take a good look around you. What is your company's atmosphere like? Is everything the way you want it to be? Is everyone happy? Do you have a Culture of excellence or a Culture of mediocrity?

Do your employees love their Mondays and can't wait to get back to work? Too many employees begin to feel sick on Sunday because they know they have only one more day of freedom before they go back to the salt mines.

Remember, Culture is what you do and how you do it. So let's break it down to see how to we can make the transition to the Culture of your dreams. If certain areas of your Culture are great—perfect. Keep it that way and focus instead on the areas that need to change.

IS YOUR CULTURE EXCITING?

Most of us like a little excitement from time to time. In our personal lives, we plan trips, vacations, holiday and birthday celebrations, and a special meal once in a while. If we get lazy and don't shake things up now and again, life seems boring.

Since we create excitement for ourselves in our off time, it seems only natural to be free to break up the monotony of doing the same thing day after day at our jobs, too.

When was the last time you had a potluck at work? It doesn't cost anything if everyone chips in. When was the last time you went on a field trip inside or outside the company? You may not get much work done, but you will surely increase communication and build relationships—resulting in improved teamwork.

Does everyone celebrate birthdays? At my clinic, every patient got a birthday card from us; we let them know they were special and they got a free visit! I can't tell you how many times patients told me the card was the first they received that year; for some of them, it was the only card they received. Remember, everybody matters, and we need to demonstrate that again and again. A card or small present may make someone's day.

Plan to put a little excitement in the lives of everyone at work. It's a minimal investment that leads to energized employees. And that excitement will spill over to your customers as well.

My friend Brad Pierce and his restaurant supply company, Restaurant Equipment World, have been going gangbusters.

I first met Brad during his visit to Zappos, and he told me that his family-owned company had leveled off after 37 years. Brad and I talked for a long time and kept in touch, and he went on to implement the ideas we discussed—the very ideas I'm sharing in this book.

The results have been spectacular. His company has been growing 50 percent year over year in an industry that has been down at least 40 percent over that time. Brad bought a new plane to travel to his customers so he could create better relationships by talking with them in person. And in the process he has created a great company Culture and allowed his employees to be part of the success. He makes it fun. He has expanded his U.S. operations and is branching out internationally with an office in Dubai.

Once when we were talking on the phone, Brad mentioned that his employees were at an indoor rock-climbing park. A month before that, he and his staff had gone to a pottery workshop to throw clay. When Brad decided to open his office in Dubai, he took some of his staff with him. He didn't have to; he could have saved the money, but he said it was worth every penny. Now everyone is fired up to open the new office.

Brad has the Culture of his dreams and, because of it, he and his employees have the job and company of their dreams.

Let's talk about some different aspects of Cultures. These don't represent the entire picture. They're more akin to taking your shoes off before entering your home; it's just part of the way you live.

A CULTURE OF SALUTATIONS

How do you greet each other at work? Is there a warm "Hello" when passing your coworkers, or do you keep your head down and rush to your desk? A greeting may seem like a little thing, but over time it can take on huge significance. A smile and a genuine "How are you?" or "Nice to see you" goes miles in anyone's book.

Would you really want to work at a place where no one smiles or acknowledges your existence?

How do your employees greet guests and customers?

As an invited guest to many businesses, I have often been completely ignored. Literally, no one greeted me when I arrived. Even though I could see 30 employees within 50 feet, no one looked up, or if they did, they looked away. Boy, would I love to work there—not! On occasion, when I have arrived on time for appointments and waited for 15 minutes without anyone showing up (including the person I was supposed to meet), I've left and never gone back. The message of the Culture was evident: "Ignore anyone you don't recognize, or if you can't ignore them, make them wait." I bet that if they ignore guests, they ignore customers, and they probably don't treat each other very well.

A CULTURE OF TRADITIONS

Do all the employees know your company history and what it took to get to where you are? Are there traditions within your company that employees can look forward to? Traditions help unify a group and give everyone a sense of belonging. Acknowledging and celebrating traditions fuels your employees' self-esteem.

At Zappos we had an annual head-shaving tradition. It didn't have any noble purpose. Someone just thought it up one year, we did it, and then it became a tradition. And since summertime in Las Vegas reaches 115 degrees outside, it was a refreshing tradition! Almost everyone participated, and those who chose not to weren't left out; they could get their hair dyed with Zappos' blue hair paint that washes out. The event created a sense of solidarity and a feeling that we were part of something special. The tradition also aligned with at least three of our core Values:

Build a Positive Team and Family Spirit

Create Fun and a Little Weirdness

Be Adventurous, Creative, and Open-Minded

And I guess those who shaved their heads or cut off most of their hair also adhered to one other Value: Do More With Less.

A CULTURE OF CREATION AND INNOVATION—CALL A "TIME-OUT"

Does your staff have the freedom to add value to what you make? Are your Vision and Purpose blueprints for creativity?

How many times have your employees heard the words, "No," "Don't," or "You can't"?

Many companies fail to stay current with the wants, needs, and demands of the employee and customer. Teams and departments often just keep doing what they're doing; they don't stop to innovate. It's not on purpose. It's just that most of the time our priorities get messed up. People get so immersed working *in* the business that they neglect working *on* the Business.

It's the same with our personal lives. We get so busy doing things *in* our lives, we lose focus on working *on* our lives. Often we look up and realize that we have forgotten things that are truly important, like our health. Have you ever been so busy that you suddenly wake up and find you haven't exercised like you used to—or, more exactly, that you haven't done anything in the past year or two—and are two sizes bigger than you used to be? Have you been so busy that you have eaten not from the garden but on the run, with a lot of meals coming from fast-food joints?

Have you been so busy that you can't even remember the last couple of years of your kid's life? Are your friends—the ones who used to be close—just distant memories?

Well, that's what goes on in business, too. As I said, we get so busy working *in* the business that we forget to take time to work *on* the business.

Sometimes we need to take a time-out to reassess our priorities and identify what is truly important. Are we in alignment with the Information Age and the wants, needs, and demands of employees or customers? Are our Unique/WOW Factors up to date? Is the company aligned with the Vision and Purpose? Even more crucial, is our Vision and Purpose up to date and still attracting employees and customers? Once we've ascertained these things, we can make it a point in the future to "check yourself, before you wreck yourself . . . and your business."

At Zappos, time-outs often were valuable for the teams and departments I met with. Since the employees were the experts at what they did, and were the best ones to figure out ways to improve things, they needed to have the time to do just that.

Thanks to those time-outs, employees would come up with some great ideas. They knew that they had to take the company to the Next Level. After eight years, for example, we didn't want to be doing things the way we did them in year two. Time and time again, staff members figured out how to improve efficiency or automate processes.

Why wait for commands to come down from the top when we already had the freedom to innovate as part of our Culture? It may sound counterintuitive, but sometimes, all you need to do to take things to the Next Level is to call a time-out.

A CULTURE OF LEADERSHIP

Does your company have great leaders who have the opportunity—and regard it as their duty—to help others become leaders? Does your company mentor employees so that they can reach their potential? Or do you have suffocating managers who tell grown-up people what to do and how to do it? Yikes!

The next section goes into leadership in detail, so that you can help empower your employees to take their lives to the Next Level, and they will take the company to the Next Level as well!

A CULTURE OF PLANNING

Does your company have a well-thought-out plan to grow, or do decision makers shoot from the hip? In underdeveloped countries with poor transportation planning, carts, donkeys, bikes, motorcycles, buses, and cars all compete for the same lanes. Result: gridlock. Does that sound like your company? Or is there a blueprint for all to follow?

A CULTURE OF EMPLOYEES

To keep your company's Culture strong, no matter what your Culture is, you should hire employees who embrace your Vision, Purpose, and Values. That way, everyone gets along, and a team spirit keeps things moving forward.

As we've noted, you can bring in the rock stars, but if they are not in alignment with your Values, and they don't get along with others, your company won't progress. Does everyone need to have "exactly" the same attitude and share the "exact" same values that frame your Culture? No, of course not, because we are all different and unique. But they shouldn't be too far off base, either. Look at your friends; most likely, they share the same general attitudes and Values you do, though some may be more dynamic and engaging than others.

A CULTURE OF MIND-SET

So what is the mind-set of your Culture? Is it what you really want? Does it align with the outcome you desire? If not, you can transform your employees' mind-set over time, beginning with articulating Values.

What makes up a positive mind-set? In my experience, executives and employees all come up with the same list of ideal qualities:

- Getting things done
- Figuring things out
- Taking it to the Next Level
- "Spin it & Win it"
- The bigger the challenge the more fun it is

At Zappos, our attitudes encompassed all of the above to make up what I called the "Spin it & Win it" mind-set. Whenever we were faced with a challenge, we turned it into a positive, an opportunity, or a lesson. Here's what happened a month before I left the company.

An employee came by to see me, and while we chatted, she sat on the Throne. I noticed that she had a fresh plaster cast on her left leg. "It looks like you broke your ankle," I said. "I am so sorry. What a terrible thing!"

She didn't blink. "Are you kidding, Doc?" she said. "I Spin it & Win it; the other ankle is just perfect."

With a Spin it & Win it mind-set, you can overcome any obstacle and conquer anything. Trust me, it works.

And it's easy for the attitude to spread. After I gave a talk at the Adidas headquarters, the company embroidered Adidas hats with the saying "Spin it & Win it" on them for all their employees to wear.

Is your Culture being passed on to the next generation?

A popular definition of the word *culture* is "the predominating attitudes and behavior that characterize the functioning of a group or organization and the development of the intellect through training or education that leads to enlightenment." What happens, though, as the original members of the group begin to get older? A great Culture requires a conscious effort to ensure that it's transmitted from generation to generation.

Consider the Shakers. The religious group, which was formed in 18th-century England, received high praise for frugality, honesty, and other virtues, yet parts of the Shaker culture held back the group's growth.

First, men and women lived apart from each other and did everything separately. They practiced celibacy, so the only way there could be a new generation was to adopt children. At the peak of the Shaker movement in America, in 1840, there were 6,000 members, but by 2009 only 5 remained. The Culture was admirable, yet the Business Model—not reproducing—did not sustain them in the long term.

The workforce of today is not made up of the same folks as 20 years ago. Yes, there are employees from older generations, but the majority is now Gen Y and Millennials. They have been raised differently from baby boomers and expect different things. These younger employees have grown up with the Internet and text messaging. They're adept at social networking and don't tolerate poor work environments for long. They certainly don't want to experience what their parents have—work for 40 years and then watch your retirement savings disappear. Today their choices of where to work are many, and the news—good and bad—about a company's Culture and work environment spreads more quickly than ever. It's increasingly important therefore to make sure the Culture is passed on to the next generation and that it evolves with the new wants, needs, and demands of the employees and customers, while keeping your company's DNA intact.

Culture is the feeling of community and being part of something.

One young lady at Zappos told me how the Culture there changed her family's life. I had gotten to know her over a period of time, and together we had set some goals. One day she came into my office, wriggled onto the throne, and said, "Doc, I need to tell you a story."

"Remember about a year ago," she began, "when we first talked and I told you I was unsure about taking the job here at Zappos? I had also applied for a county job that paid twice as much. I have two teenage boys to take care of by myself, and I could use the extra dough.

"Well, the phone rang yesterday afternoon, and my 16-year-old picked it up and said, 'No thank you. She is working at Zappos and doesn't need that job anymore.'

"I was flabbergasted and asked my son, 'Who was that?' He answered, 'Mom, that was the person at the county job you applied for, but I told her no, because you have never been happier, and we have never been happier as a family since you started working for Zappos. And we don't need the money that bad.'"

Can you imagine a teenage boy saying that? It highlights the effects of a super Culture, not only at work but on the home scene as well. It brought tears to my eyes.

Increase the performance of your people, and you will increase the performance of your company.

As we've noted, 50 percent of S&P companies in the 1950s were not around in 1970. And 50 percent of companies in 1970 were gone by the

1990s. What happened? The Cultures that didn't foster creativity or innovation didn't evolve with the times.

When you see that your company is not moving in the right direction, it's time to transform your Culture. Changing the way you act and behave is necessary to get what you want.

You've probably seen the commercial about California cheese that ends with the slogan, "Happy cows make happy cheese." Behind the animals, the backdrop shows idyllic meadows and rolling hills. You're meant to see a correlation between treating the cows nicely and producing a better product. Surely we wouldn't want our cheese to come from cows that are cooped up in cramped stalls with no grass in sight.

An unassociated study revealed another interesting fact: treating cows nicely actually resulted in greater milk production. Researchers at Newcastle University in the United Kingdom studied the working relationship between farmers and dairy cows. They found that farmers who gave their cows TLC and more personal attention reaped the benefits of increased milk production over a ten-month period. On average, a cow produces about 1,981 gallons of milk during this span. But, strange as this may sound, by referring to their cattle by name, farmers got 68 gallons more milk yield, per cow, from their herd. Scientists have concluded that personal attention improves cows' comfort level while lessening their fear of human contact.

Now, people are not cattle, so the analogy goes only so far. But don't you think that people will be more creative and deliver a better end product if they are treated nicely?

What's in a name?

We have three cats: Two of them are two years old, and the third, Nellie, is nine. She has always been an angry cat, and we call her the "spinster." She swipes at the other cats when she gets the chance, and because of her attitude, we don't pay much attention to her. But when Nellie was a kitten, she took a liking to our youngest boy, Sam, who was then 2 years old. Nellie sleeps with Sam and completely adores him.

The other night my wife and I were talking about how Nellie wasn't friendly, and Sam, who's now 13, took us to task. "She's a friendly cat," he insisted. "You just have to be nice to her and pet her, call her by her name and not 'spinster,' and she is nice back." Sam had described perfectly the concept of reciprocation, using the example of a household pet.

So how are you treating your employees? Do you call them by name? Do you know where they were born, what they did after high school, where they live, whom they live with, or what they are passionate about? Do you recognize them as human beings? Or do you just regard them as moneymakers for the company? If management treats employees like they matter, asking about their personal lives and acknowledging what is important to them, reciprocation occurs—it's human nature. And you will have the Culture and company of your dreams.

The Culture is the "glue"

By creating a great Culture, your group, team, or organization will thrive. If you surround your employees with all of the positive attributes that a great Culture can offer, the foundation is set for everyone to be happy and empowered, proud to be a part of the company and eager for it to thrive.

Yes, Culture is what you do, why you do it, and how you do it, along with the language, beliefs, thoughts, decisions, and actions of your organization. Culture holds everything together; it is the glue, and without it the organization would revert to separate individuals out only for themselves. When that happens, employees and the company take off in directions not originally intended.

By now, hopefully, it's apparent that Culture is the apex of the structure built with Vision, Purpose, Business Model, Unique/WOW Factors, and Values. We've followed the blueprint to this point. What's the next step? It's time to add the interior design elements that will make our businesses great places to work, to create, and to generate experiences that connect us emotionally to our customers—and them to us!

This Is Empowering and Passing the Torch—Leadership

Leadership:
The position of a leader or the person heading a group;
the capacity to lead—that is, to guide on a way; direct
the activity of; go at the head of.

Managing is *not* leading

Leadership plays a huge role in empowering employees and keeping the structural foundations of the corporate Culture in place. If leadership is handled properly, employees can bring the Culture to life . . . and then help pass the torch to the next generation.

A note of caution, though. Leadership comes from within management, yet many times no one within management is truly leading—only managing. There is a difference between leadership and management. As the saying goes: lead people and manage things (like numbers and processes).

This may seem like splitting hairs, but it is important to make the distinction between leaders and managers and between leadership and management. They are related, but each has distinct characteristics.

Imagine the leader of a call center. This leader is within management because he *manages* all the processes, such as call volume, answer time, metrics, and so on. He is also within the leadership because he *leads* the employees to best arrive at the metrics that are desired. Many companies don't understand this simple difference.

And some companies compound the problem with managers nicknamed "Boss" who micromanage employees. I have never met anyone who liked to be managed or bossed. I'm appalled when employees tell me they have to do this or can't do that because their boss won't let them.

Are you a boss or a leader?

I have had weekend golf games spoiled because a friend's boss threw a week's worth of work on my friend's desk on a Friday afternoon and told him that the assignment needed to be ready for a presentation first thing Monday morning.

I have been self-employed my entire adult life—with the exception of the Zappos assignment—and I find it extremely odd to hear adults refer to a boss who tells them what to do. Is this the Soviet Union in the 1940s?

Leaders don't tell people what to do; they let them know what needs to be done and help them if necessary.

Managers have power *over* people, and leaders have power *with* people; as I've noted, you can manage money but you cannot manage people.

Does the management in your company foster a "chain of command" or a "chain of empowerment"?

I believe that most people would choose a leader who empowers them instead of having a manager or boss. What do you have in your company: someone telling you to what to do all day? Or someone who is inspiring and empowering your employees?

GREAT LEADERS HAVE A POSITIVE IMPACT ON ANY TEAM

Companies that have weathered economic storms and stood the test of time have done so because of great leaders. They are the ones who direct the activity of the staff and company. Just as in a jungle expedition, there may be many obstacles along the way; it is up to the leader to keep everyone safe until the end of the trip.

A great leader is a steward of the people being led. A captain of a plane or ship makes sure all the passengers are safe before leaving the craft. That's what they signed up for. The leaders of a company should do the same: guide their people safely and empower them to be the best they can be. As we discussed in the first half of this book, thanks to the shift to the Information Age and the course of recent events, people today have had enough of being ripped off. Above all, they want to be treated like they matter. In a company, that means that leaders have to treat employees well.

Happy employees lead to happy customers, which develops into a happy business. That's the cycle, in a nutshell.

And this cycle starts with the leadership of the company.

Unfortunately, you don't have to look far to find poor leadership. Countless companies from the recent past have provided great examples. At energy giant Enron, for example, the leaders knowingly made choices that ultimately brought down the company. In the 1980s the decisions of Charles H. Keating, chairman of Lincoln Savings & Loan, led to the collapse of the savings and loan industry. More recently the mistakes of executives of Lehman Brothers, a global financial services firm, affected the stability of the global economy.

Most failed companies have one thing in common: it was the choices and actions of their leadership—not the employees—that caused the firms to implode. Tens of thousands of employees made up the workforce of these giant failed corporations, but it was usually the deeds of only a handful that brought about their downfall.

The results are heartbreaking. Not only are those employees out of work (and many times out of their retirement savings), but also ten times that many investors in public companies have seen their nest eggs vanish.

The repercussions of the decisions of corporate leaders have affected entire nations. Therefore, leaders have a very real and serious duty to perform wisely, for the effects of their decisions are far-reaching indeed.

If employees are engaged, empowered, and directed by their leaders, future generations of employees and leadership will be able to maintain the corporate Culture that underlies its success. Leadership is the crucial starting point or foundation of this cycle.

We have all seen great leadership in action. Take professional sports, which is a business. The teams with the best leadership are the teams that win. Leaders pick the players, empower the players, and coach players winning ways. And year after year, you can see the results in the win column.

Corporations that keep growing and remain on *Fortune's* "Best Places to Work" list also are the beneficiaries of great leadership. Many companies don't understand this. Creating a better work environment is the first step in creating a business that will stand the test of time. It all begins with leaders guided by a great Vision and Purpose, leading people and managing things.

There is no one best way to lead

As Zappos grew, we wanted to make sure the management-level staff had all the necessary tools to help them be the best they could be. We also wanted to nurture leaders from within the company and to develop a consistent style of leadership, while recognizing that there are different ways to lead.

I was tapped to create leadership training, and I created a three-hour workshop, which I delivered to every management-level employee we had at the time. Of course, I titled it "Dr. Vik's Leadership Essentials."

Before we started each workshop, I asked all the attendees to identify themselves and let everyone know what they considered their best leadership skill. One by one, these future Zappos leaders stood up and gave their names and what they did. Some described their best leadership quality as "listening"; others said "being involved in the process." The list went on: they "asked questions," "were empathetic," "set goals," or "got to know every team member personally." In each workshop, once we had gone all around the room, we had a list of at least 20 different leadership qualities.

Through this exercise everyone understood that there is no one way to lead or empower others. People are free to choose their best leadership style as long as they empower the people they work with and guide them to be the best they can be.

Below is a list of great leadership qualities. You can add your own definitions as well.

1. Trustworthiness
2. Takes ownership
3. Listening

4. Sincerity

5. Caring

(Notice that there is no mention on the list of gossiping, choosing sides, or raising your voice.)

A leadership hall of horrors

Before we learn more about what makes a great leader, perhaps we'd do well to know what enemies we might encounter in workplaces where employees, not processes, are being managed. I'll never forget what one Leadership Essentials Workshop attendee told me when I asked, "What did your worst manager do to make him- or herself the worst?" The answer? "My old boss threw a lamp at me."

IVORY TOWER LEADERSHIP

I have seen this type of "managing," as opposed to leading, time and time again. It occurs when leaders think they are better than their employees, or they just don't care to be bothered. They simply don't make time for those they view as minions.

You know the ivory tower leaders: they have separate and secluded offices. I've even heard stories of executive offices that required a special access key. That certainly keeps all the riffraff (otherwise known as employees) out. You can't get to see the leaders, let alone have a conversation with them. They just lock themselves away from employees, when in truth employees are the heart and soul of a business—especially when it comes to creation and invention. What a joke!

> **If those at the top in your company want only to manage employees, instead of leading and empowering them, you will be powerless to change things unless there is a coup!**

If the top decision-makers never communicate with employees, you can't do much about transforming their management style. If top executives are sequestered from everyone else, they won't even be able to hear your voice.

THE LEADERSHIP BULLY

I have firsthand experience with a CEO who's a bully. I'm not saying these leaders push people around physically, but their speech and body language bully staff members all the same. Haven't you ever heard someone say, "If you don't do what I say, there will be consequences," or "It's my way or the highway"? That's a bully.

Bullies are everywhere. In fact, this behavior has become so prevalent that there's now a national campaign against bullying. Most of us have probably encountered bullies during our school days. They're also in the workplace, but *the most dangerous place a bully can be is in the top spot in the company.*

Various types of leaders exist. Which type are you?

At one big firm I was working with, I met with an executive team to discuss corporate Culture. Before the meeting, one of the execs asked me to say to the CEO, when he joined the meeting, that being late was not good for the Culture. When the CEO came in 15 minutes late—as expected—nobody confronted him. That was his style: to arrive late and run overtime. It was sad to see those managers so afraid of the repercussions if they spoke up.

With a bully at the top, you have a Culture where little gets done. Meetings function poorly and there's a lack of collaboration. I'm not saying that a corporate dictatorship can't succeed, but it's far from a nice place to work—unless you are at the top.

I've heard "old school" leaders lament the fact that "work ethic is just not the same anymore." You've probably heard similar comments, like "when I was 25, I used to lift 100 bags up eight flights of stairs, and if I didn't move fast enough my boss would hit me." I always respond, "It doesn't look like you work there anymore." And the usual answer to that is, "Yeah, it was awful. I quit." Exactly! It wasn't right then, and it isn't right now.

LAZY-LOAF LEADERSHIP

It's usually up to an entire team to get things done, but if a leader doesn't set the tone and help execute the plan, nothing will happen.

We see this pattern all too often—from doctor's offices to Internet companies. There are people in management who won't initiate anything or even act on their company's plan. They know what needs to be done, but they just don't do much about it. Forget them. You need to model yourself after the leaders who not only do what needs to be done but who think and act one step ahead. They are the ones who will succeed.

Before you read any further, take a moment to ask yourself honestly: Am I a leader who shuns staff, bullies them, or fails to get the ball rolling? If you have ever resorted to these leadership styles, read on and see how you can change your behavior and grow your business.

Thanks for the day!

Sad to say, there are, in fact, some horrible leaders in the business world. To ensure that none of these negative behaviors creep into your organization, here are some important questions for you and your leadership team:

- Have you consistently demonstrated leadership skills?
- Have you always acknowledged and recognized your staff or have you told them how to do things?
- Do you compliment or criticize?
- Who was your best leader or mentor? Why?

I have asked many people who their most memorable mentor was. Not surprisingly, it's usually someone who helped them at school or at work, or a family member or friend. The interesting part, though, is that most people I talk to say their mentors didn't even know they had that role. They just did what they did, and it had a positive effect.

Are you guiding people by example so that they consider you their mentor? Here's one simple way to start: Thank your employees for giving their day to you. Yes, the employees are getting paid, but increasingly people have a choice of where they want to spend most of their waking hours. When they choose your company, they should be thanked for it. After all, they set alarms in the morning and plan their entire life—kids' activities, get-togethers, health appointments, and everything else—around their work.

Thanks for the day!

When I "retired" from my clinic, my staff gave me a trophy engraved with the words "Thanks for the Day." It choked me up when they presented it to me, even more when they said they wanted to thank me because at the end of every day, I had thanked them for coming to work and giving their day to the clinic and to our patients.

I believe most companies would have a much better Culture if the leaders simply thanked their employees every day. Just because workers get paid, it doesn't negate the fact that they want to be thanked for their contribution.

Here are some other points to get you thinking about great leadership:

- Have you taken sole responsibility for your employees' growth?
- Are you a caring authority figure?
- Do you motivate by your own actions? Or do you sit on the sidelines and bark orders?
- Are you creating leaders or managing employees?
- Does your leadership elevate your employees' lives and the lives of their families?
- Would you rather have leaders or employees work for you?
- Do you walk the walk?
- Are you using positive vocabulary to start the empowerment process with your team? (Remember . . . thoughts drive emotions, actions, and our future.)

We want the skills, talents, and attitudes of leadership to be contagious.

When the leadership is inspiring and empowering, it sets the tone of the Culture and creates the corporate DNA for future generations of employees.

Great leaders treat employees like they matter—because they do!

A friend and mentor of mine is Tom Mendoza, Vice Chairman at NetApp. Tom's a big reason the company vaulted to the top spot on *Fortune*'s list of "Best Companies to Work For." His staff enjoys the perks that progressive companies offer, but just as importantly, they are engaged by his leadership and attitude. Tom is a people person. He started as a company salesman in 1992, but his focus on taking care of employees and customers soon gained notice, and he eventually rose to be president. Now he is Vice Chairman.

Even though Tom gave $37 million to his alma mater, Notre Dame, to open up the Tom Mendoza College of Business, he knows how to connect with everyone. He tells jokes and always asks about you. He is a major reason why people like to work at NetApp.

Tom says, "People don't really care what you know, unless they know you care, and we try to show them we care a lot." All leaders should treat every employee, customer, and stakeholder as though they care, because people matter; they always have and always will.

Tom started a process at work called "Catch somebody doing something right." Whenever any employee sees someone else doing something extraordinary, they e-mail Tom and tell him. Tom calls that special staffer, wherever he or she may be in the world, and says, "I heard what you did and want to thank you for it." He makes as many as 10 to 15 calls a day to his employees around the world.

Tom has helped create quite an empowering Culture at NetApp, and he is a role model for all of us.

FOCUS ON YOUR EMPLOYEES' GREATNESS

People usually know their shortcomings, and they don't appreciate it when someone points out mistakes. At NetApp, the Culture focuses on the greatness of its people, not their challenges. As a result, employees are inspired to reach their potential. And guess what? Not only does the company benefit when it invests in its people, so do the employees.

In a sense, employers buy relationships, because companies make money with the help of others. Therefore it makes sense not to use employees for our own gain, giving little in return. Think how much more effectively those employees win over customers when their company has already won them over with recognition, acknowledgment, empowerment, and rewards?

Once again, it comes down to taking the time to get to know employees and treating them as we should.

When you shine a light on what someone is doing right, you will see more of what you like.

There is no reason to highlight mistakes or focus on what you *don't* want done. Whatever we shine a light on stays in the forefront of people's minds, so choose wisely. Do you want employees dwelling on their mistakes or trying to replicate their successes?

For a service vibe and Culture to stay strong, it must be part of a company's DNA and be passed on to future generations. The duty, responsibility, and opportunity for that lie directly with its leaders.

Teams mirror management

"Teams mirror management" is a concept similar to "Customers mirror employees." They both rely on the process of reciprocation.

If your manager agreed to speak to you in confidence, and you later found out that she had shared your private conversation, would you lose trust in her? Yes, but your reaction is really a reflection of the manager who broke the trust first.

The same goes for caring. If you have an employee who doesn't care about you, it's undoubtedly because you don't care about them.

I once coached a manager who was facing a challenge with her team. She was frustrated and at the end of her rope. "My team doesn't show up on time," she said. "They gossip about me, and they don't care what I have to say."

Then I had a talk with her team members. They said that their manager didn't listen to what they had to say, gossiped about them, and never was on time.

Unfortunately, she got what she gave.

Everything stays on course with proper leadership.

I had several discussions with this manager about where her challenges were coming from and suggested that she needed to take a good look in the mirror. Everything she was getting from her employees was a reflection of her own actions.

She needed to care more about her employees, stop her gossiping, and listen to what the team had to say to expect the same in return. She was resistant to the suggestions, however, and eventually left the company. She had reached the point of no return with her employees, and the sad thing was that she created the situation herself.

When leaders or managers are having problems with their team, they need to ask if the problems are a reflection of their own behavior.

If leaders keep taking their knowledge to the Next Level, it will spread throughout the team. Conversely, if the leaders' caring attitude starts to falter, that will show up within the team as well. Treating your employees as if they don't matter means that your customers are, essentially, getting kicked.

How can employees who are abused take care of customers any differently? The answer is *they can't*. Businesses that mistreat their employees end up chasing new customers because the old ones fire them. And with the ever-rising costs associated with the acquisition of new customers, this leads to an inevitable decline. Take care of the employees, and their success will translate to the customers.

Criticism vs. feedback—there is a difference

It is important to know the difference between criticism and feedback. Criticism is subjective and passes judgment by pointing out faults or shortcomings. It is usually received negatively because no one likes to be judged. Criticism is a de-motivator. It does not encourage anyone to perform better. Generally when people do the wrong thing, they do not need to be reprimanded. What they need is for someone to explain how to do the job correctly. This usually means, by the way, someone who is in a leadership position.

If someone didn't do something correctly, we shouldn't say, "You did this wrong, and if you do it again, we'll need to find someone else to do it." Criticism not only offends individuals but may also be interpreted as disparaging their character, especially if it includes threats and no suggestions for improvement.

Feedback, on the other hand, concentrates on what people are doing right and what needs to be done; it includes praise, approval, kindness, compliments, and support. If someone is not making their "numbers," for instance, a wise leader will say, "I can see you haven't been making your numbers. What can I do to help?"

Here's an example of how an effective leader can balance feedback so it includes an offer of help to improve a situation and acknowledgment of the employee's value.

"Jim, I know you've been with us for three years now. You've been a great employee for all that time. You come to work on time, you do what needs to be done, you are a great team player, and you are always willing to chip in. But this last project didn't quite seem to be from the real expert that you are. How do you think I can help you on this project so we can see the work that you are so famous for?"

This compliments, praises, and approves of Jim's work and his character and work ethic, and it allows Jim to look good and receive help if he wants it.

In my leadership workshops at Zappos, I asked attendees to take back to their team just one word that was positive and empowering. They were to use that word for 30 days. One of the outcomes was that the most of the teams started to use those positive words. Simply taking some vocabulary to the Next Level got things moving in a positive direction.

The greatest leaders in the world can create the greatest company in the world if they know how to spread their knowledge through the company. How?

First, they can do it by acting as role models and mentors, which will have both a direct and indirect impact on others.

Leaders don't have to "teach" in order for the team to learn; all team members have to do is watch and follow suit.

Second, true leaders will always focus their attention on the positive, using feedback and encouragement in place of criticism. A leader sets an example and allows others to act accordingly. Forced effort cannot be sustained and only leads to resistance. A leader allows his or her employees to make mistakes and to learn from them. You can't expect the best at the beginning. We are not born with perfect judgment; that's learned from experience.

Remember, most things are difficult before they become easy. If you are right-handed, for instance, try to draw with your left hand. On your first attempt, most likely, the results will be poor, but with practice, over time, the pictures will improve. A good leader understands this process.

Are we building this company for our grandchildren?

Without leaders there would be chaos, but a leader's most important job is actually to help others develop their full potential. Leaders lead by example, getting people and teams to rise to any task. Leaders are the organization's catalysts, and it is they who show other how things are done:

> **Which of your leaders are ensuring that the corporate DNA is passed down to future generations?**

> **And what exactly is being passed down?**

A great leader empowers employees to want to do something rather than be required to do something. Occasionally, of course, people need convincing, and that is where proper leadership skills come in.

> **A leader has to empower employees and inspire them to duplicate the leader's example.**

Whatever the Culture is within the company, the leader should be a model for the next generation of leaders to follow. Otherwise a firm's accumulated knowledge will be lost. And the Vision, Purpose, Values, and other keys to the company's Culture will disappear.

MOST PEOPLE WANT TO LEARN, BUT DON'T WANT TO BE TAUGHT

It is important for a leader to keep in mind that people generally are eager to learn, but they're not looking for the rote memorization we may have experienced in school. Adults want to learn in a creative, empowering, and inspiring way, and providing that is the responsibility, duty and opportunity of every leader within every organization.

When leaders act as positive role models and get involved in some task, employees are much less resistant to the work. That doesn't mean that a leader has to be there every step of the way; allowing employees to do it themselves will still produce the best results. Involvement can mean checking on progress at regular intervals and being available to answer questions. It's that simple. No one likes to take orders from someone on the sidelines.

"But, as a leader," you might argue, "sometimes I don't have the time to get that involved." Leaders cannot lead anyone or anything by staying in their offices. They must be part of the process and out in front, and their skills are revealed by the way they guide others. What I have heard over and over again is that a person is a great leader because he or she would never ask someone to do something they wouldn't do themselves.

If you empower people to take responsibility for their own growth and allow them to reach their potential, you are truly a leader.

Leaders need to empower their employees to be creative.

Here's a great example: An employee of a national pizza company invented his own dish at one of the restaurants in Ohio. After it became a favorite with the local customers, he submitted his idea to management, and now it is part of the chain's menu nationally. Empowerment for the employee equals more profits for the company. Win–win.

Leadership follows from a clear compelling Vision and Purpose. In those cases, as we've noted, you don't need to tell employees what to do because they know what needs to be done. It's the workers, after all, who have their fingers on the pulse of the business. And if they are allowed to do so, employees are really good at figuring things out, trust me. If they're free to create, they may come up with something better than you hoped for, and they have a stake in its success. And if they swerve a little off track, you can suggest things to help them get back on course with a gentle nudge.

UPS provides a terrific illustration of employees figuring out how to become more efficient, save resources, and decrease the world carbon footprint, almost 100 years after the company was founded as the American Messenger Company in 1907.

UPS—NO LEFT TURNS

In 2004, after evaluating its CO_2 emissions, UPS announced that its drivers would avoid making left turns. The company calculated that reducing the amount of time spent idling while waiting to make left turns would save millions of dollars in fuel costs every year.

They were right. In 2006, UPS trucks drove 2.5 billion miles. The company estimated that, thanks to its unique package-flow technology combined with the right-turn routes, they'd also saved 28.5 million miles, and three million gallons of fuel. Talk about improving the bottom line!

> **If we just keep telling employees what to do, they are trained to do only what we tell them.**

Three keys to great leadership

Why become a leader? When I ask that question, most people respond that they want to help people, just the way they've been helped in their past. So if you are a leader, helping and empowering people are the primary goals.

A leader can raise the employees' expectations of themselves, reinforcing their abilities and getting them closer to their full potential. Leaders also embrace the positive, which allows them to be effective and inspirational role models.

Like a great coach, a great leader allows people to empower themselves with a positive mind-set about their abilities.

There are three important keys to becoming a successful leader: self-improvement, communication, and relationships.

SELF-IMPROVEMENT

Employees can match a leader's knowledge and capabilities, but it may be difficult for them to surpass them. So to keep the company advancing, a leader should be working on self-improvement, too.

When leaders take the initiative to better themselves, they can pass along their new knowledge and wisdom to the entire team. As we said before, teams mirror management, so to ensure your team is taking things to the Next Level, the leader has to take the first step.

> Leaders must rely on their own self-improvement in order to keep the team moving forward.

> Figure out what you need to do to empower yourself, then, in turn, empower your team. Your team is a reflection of you, and you want that reflection to shine as bright as the sun.

COMMUNICATION

As we've said in the Culture section, proper communication is crucial to any organization. It can unite a team and help it accomplish great things, but a disconnect in communication can actually lead to the downfall of a company.

Unfortunately, fast-growing companies frequently experience problems in communication. It's a common scenario. Communication starts out great at a company's beginning, when everyone can hear the message directly from the leader. As the firm grows, however, the voice of the leader becomes fainter, and employees can misinterpret it. A solid blueprint that details the company's Culture helps tremendously, but too often no one takes the time to see that the blueprint is in place.

> *Great leaders create relationships that focus on the success of others.*

And once an organization begins to be organized into teams or divisions, it's easy for them isolate themselves, breaking down communication and relationships even more.

As we've noted, weekly executive meetings are an effective way to keep communication open and the Culture intact.

Communication is a two-way street

A little small talk can create big results. Great leaders ask their employees about family, life, goals, and interests. If they really care, employees understand that the leaders are concerned not just about work but about really knowing them. That's what leaders do. Ask about spouses, children, and hobbies. Call employees by name. (Our names are the sweetest words we can hear!) In turn, employees will to get to know their leader. Of course, if a leader doesn't care about the people in the company, don't expect the workers to care about their leader—or their customers, for that matter.

Personalizing communication is important. When you say, "Nice job," it may sound good to you, but that's a rather broad statement. Something more personalized would better empower an employee. Why not, "Mary, I noticed that report you wrote. It was one of the most detailed and professional reports I have ever seen. Thank you so much, I am very proud of you, and you should be very proud of yourself too." That kind of praise will be much more effective, and chances are your employees will repeat the comment and spread the love.

People, especially leaders, should listen twice as much as they speak; that's why, as the old adage says, we were born with two ears and one mouth. In listening we not only learn others' points of view, we show that we are interested in what they have to say. People love to talk about themselves, but leaders not only have to listen, they also have to hear what people say. There is a difference.

Leaders listen more than they talk and they hear what is said.

Here are some other great communication tips:

- Use "we," "ours," and "us" more than "me" or "I." Words like these emphasize a team spirit and indicate that we're all in this together.

- Use employees' names. Believe me, one's name sounds 10,000 times better than anything else. And don't forget salutations: Say "Hello" and "Good-bye."

- Communicate promptly—inside and outside the company— whether by e-mail, phone calls, or one-on-one chats.

- Be interested. People are flattered when you show them attention.

- Listen without distraction.

It doesn't always have to be personal

Yes, you should personalize acknowledgment and recognition, but when it comes to giving direction, it's better to be impersonal. That way, a remark can be heard more objectively.

For instance, if you say to an employee, "I want you to do it this way," the person will probably react with resistance, because there's a tinge of "do it my way or take the highway."

Why not say, "We usually do it this way. What do you think?" The employee is less likely to take offense at that. The nudging and the direction come across as objective, with the undertone of "This is the way the company does it. It's not just all about me."

Leaders don't argue to try to make their point. They know that no one ever truly wins an argument. Even though you might think you came out on top, you haven't. Buddha said it best: "Hatred is never ended by hatred, but by love."

Look in a person's left eye while you talk and listen

We see with our eyes, but most of our neural pathways don't go to the same side of our brains. The nerves cross over to the opposite side. So most of the left eye's information goes to our right brain; most of our right eye's information heads to the left side of the brain.

Now, the left brain is logical, analytical, rational, and objective—basically, it judges. The right brain, however, is intuitive, subjective. It's the creative side.

So when we look into someone's left eye, the person receives the information in the nonjudgmental part of the brain. That suggests that you are communicating from the heart. People feel it and know it, even if they can't explain it.

The next time you want to really communicate with someone, focus your attention on the left eye. The person will almost always lock onto what you're saying, and you will connect as you've never connected before. This works extremely well with kids, when you focus on their left eyes; it is amazing what happens.

RELATIONSHIPS

If leaders need employees to care about the company, leaders must start by caring about their employees. Think of it as paying it forward. A relationship goes both ways; there has to be give-and-take. You help me and I'll help you. I care about you and you care about me.

Relationships are fostered by focusing on what we can do for others. Over time, they'll reciprocate.

How do you feel about people who call or communicate only when they want or need something? Do you go the extra mile for them? No, not usually.

Relationships thrive on acknowledgment and recognition. We've all heard that employees don't quit their company, they quit their boss. Why? Usually because acknowledgment and recognition were nowhere to be had, so the employee feels there is no real purpose or reason for him or her to be there. Showing your gratitude to employees will not only fulfill their needs, it will demonstrate to others what kind of work earns accolades; it's another win–win.

Taking a sincere and genuine interest in others creates rapport and builds leadership.

People matter, and when you show them that you care who they are and what they have to say, you will energize them. Leaders are not afraid to give out praise or to pass along a compliment. Even small talk shows that you recognize someone as an individual and an asset to the company.

It's all a matter of perspective

With the exponential expansion of choices at everyone's fingertips, the old way of doing business just won't do. People no longer settle for the traditional boss–employee dynamic in which grown men and women are told what to do by an executive who tries to manage rather than lead them. No more "powerful and powerless." No need to enter a workplace filled with orders, rules, and restrictions. No more being told what to do and when to do it. Those days are over.

When it comes to assessing performance, however, everyone has a slightly different point of view.

FROM AN EMPLOYEE'S PERSPECTIVE

Employees usually view their leader as the one in control of advancement. A leader's approval is needed to receive a raise, for example, which may mean a newer car, an upgrade in living arrangements, that dreamed-of vacation. The only thing in the way of those perks is the leader. So employees don't take the review process lightly, and neither should the leader.

It's the leaders' duty to develop the people in their charge, and if employees do not improve, leaders bear responsibility for that.

An employee may also see a leader's assessment as subjective and not as helpful for advancement as it might be.

FROM THE LEADER'S PERSPECTIVE

Other managers have told me that "Employees should just do as they are told," or more succinctly, they should "shut up and get to work." Those attitudes are a relic of days gone by.

In my younger years, I worked in construction as a framer. My boss would yell, "I want to see asses and elbows," which meant that if we were doing our jobs properly, we'd be bending over and nailing the studs to the bottom and top plate. All he would see would be our asses in the air and our elbows swinging the hammer. But that was the old way.

Leaders understand that their point of view may differ from that of employees, and that they should make an effort to bridge the gap.

They should also understand that they're responsible for giving the employees support and empowerment so they can advance. If no one is improving, that is partly the leader's fault. How a team is doing is a reflection of the leader.

A leader understands that everyone is someone's child, brother, sister, father, or mother and that they need to be objective and avoid even the perception of subjectivity.

Great leaders can have a positive impact on someone's life at work and at home.

And objectivity is paramount in all interactions with employees to promote a high level of trust and to counteract any perception of favoritism.

FROM AN OUTSIDE PERSPECTIVE

A leader will be judged by outsiders on the team's result, because that's mostly what outsiders see. But leaders also have to realize that what they say has far-reaching consequences. We have all been reprimanded by someone at work, and taken that comment home. Family and friends all got a piece of our resentment. So, too, compliments or approval reach beyond the company, spreading good will to those at home.

All these elements go into producing great leadership. But others in the company—those responsible for human empowerment—also have a tremendous impact in achieving success.

This Is the Group of Champions— Human Resources or Human Empowerment

Human Empowerment can champion the Culture
to be the Shining Star.

Human Resources—HR—rocks (so stop throwing stones at them)

I don't know about you, but I love HR. The department does so much for the company and its employees, and a lot of it, I feel, goes unrecognized. I don't know how those staff members keep all the plates spinning as they constantly help folks to be their best.

HR personnel secure benefit packages for us and our families and handle our 401Ks and retirement plans. They help guarantee that we'll be safe and taken care of. Many times they oversee training, employee development, and work activities and not only during business hours.

As far as I'm concerned, they should be the most revered employees of the company.

When I directed my clinics from 1982 to 2004, I took care of all kinds of people, but at least half of our patients worked, in some capacity, in a technology company in the Silicon Valley. I would always study patient demographics—where they came from, age, profession, and so on.

HE—
Human
Empowerment

After a couple of years, I had a fair amount of data about the percentages of patients in various occupations. The stats didn't change much over the years. But the demographics that didn't seem to make sense to me were the number of teachers and HR employees.

My clinic saw some patients with trauma from accidents, but for the most part, they came in for stress-related conditions—mental, postural, or repetitive in nature. The stress often manifested itself in migraines and other headaches, as well as neck, low back, and shoulder problems. Those teachers and HR folks were some of the nicest people I have ever met, and I'd never thought of their professions as stressful, but something was certainly taking a toll!

Why were they so stressed out that they had physical symptoms? Was it because high demands were placed upon them? Were they overworked and underpaid? Teachers, I could figure out. I have kids, and I go bonkers once in a while. I can't imagine dealing with 30 of them together all day long. With the responsibility and challenge of inspiring and motivating students all with different levels of needs, it's understandable that their work can be stressful. (Teachers, I love you—and a big thank-you for all that you do!)

So that left the HR employees, and I started asking them about their job. In a nutshell, this is what they told me: the majority of their day was spent hearing "he said/she said" disagreements that had escalated out of control. They were undergoing a lot of tension and stress.

How can that be? These men and women were working with adults, helping them out, and they ended up being referees in he said/she said arguments?

My HR patients also said they had an undeserved bad rap.

I don't doubt that. Consider this scenario: a coworker or your manager tells you to go to HR. What would your reaction be? You'd probably be sure your job was about to end. The initials "HR" evoke certain unpleasant responses from everyone who hears them. It's like being told in grammar school, "You need to go to the Principal's office."

Why does everyone panic when faced with going to HR? By definition, that office should be seen as a place to get support or aid. Human Resources: Human— consisting of people; Resources—a source of supply, support, or aid. An employee who is asked to go to HR should not be scared out of his or her wits.

The use of HR as a department sprang up in the 1960s. Originally termed "human resource development," it was designed to *maximize* human potential. Yet today, even though most people within HR work very hard at the original idea, they still get an undeserved bad rap.

What is your HR department doing to change its negative connotation?

It's tough for HR to shed its connotations, though aligning itself with the goals of supplying support and maximizing human potential would be a good place to expand. So how can you change the way your employees view HR?

Since the very name HR gets in the way of accurate perceptions, why not begin by changing the name? Even though it may sound silly, a name change can do a great deal for people and companies alike.

To me, HR should be viewed more like what it is and can be: a combination of a loving, caring, empowering department that helps take employees to the Next Level, and a concierge. Changing the title to *Human Empowerment*—HE— gives the department a fresh start.

The new name will help employees focus their thoughts, decisions, and actions on empowerment, just as having a clear Vision and Purpose aligns the company and moves everyone in the same direction.

Much of what the HR department does for employees lies behind the scenes and goes unrecognized or unacknowledged. That's the reason why at Zappos we started to have the different people from HR sit in with other teams and departments. This created close relationships and increased communication companywide. Getting them front and center did wonders for everyone, especially the HR department!

The new Human Empowerment Department—HE

What if your new HE department was always asking employees if they needed anything or if there was anything they could do to help? That would be taking a proactive stance toward building relationships.

> HE can have the biggest impact on the empowerment of the employees when it acts proactively.

> Allow your HE department to empower your human assets and your Culture.

> HE can be the single biggest champion of your company's Culture. After all, they are the ones who have the relationships with and trust of the employees.

The HE Department can really help out with the Culture and brand, because if the company's Culture is shining on the inside, the brand that people outside see will shine as well.

COACHING IS A GREAT WAY TO DEFUSE ANY CHALLENGES

At Zappos, the coaching program usually was able to handle all challenges before they escalated, which turned out to be fantastic, although it wasn't planned that way. As the Coach, I would have office hours, and at least 20 employees a day stopped by to have a chat.

They knew that the Coach's office was a safe spot where they wouldn't be judged. Employees could sit on the Throne and feel like royalty. My office was a neutral zone like Switzerland. Nothing would be divulged unless the employee was going to hurt him- or herself or someone else, and that never happened.

Guys and gals would mostly come in to sort out problems in their personal lives and occasionally to talk about challenges at work. Often employees would simply "vent." My wife gave me some advice early on that really helped. "When people come to you," she said, "most of the time they just want to be heard. So don't try to fix things; just listen." For the most part, that's what I did: listen. And my rule was this: if I did talk, I wouldn't offer answers; I'd just help them with their questions.

It worked out pretty well. Over time employees came to talk not about their challenges but about solutions. And if they didn't, I would give them a nudge in that direction.

Usually after about 15 minutes of talking things over out loud, they would slap the arms of the Throne and say, "Wow, I sure feel better!" And many times I'd never said a word. I just listened and nodded and gave employees an opportunity to figure out a great solution for themselves. So in the end, the challenges didn't escalate, they were turned into solutions.

All of these coaching sessions went a long way toward empowering our employees, or more precisely, toward our employees empowering themselves. As a matter of fact, one day someone in HR took me by surprise when she said, "Doc, HR loves you!"

"What?" I said, startled.

"We love having a Coach," she went on. "We don't get the messy stuff to deal with that we would otherwise get if the challenges weren't talked out earlier."

Pretty cool. I never planned to have that outcome from coaching, but I'm sure glad I did.

What helped employees get comfortable with talking candidly about their everyday issues was a 30-day goal-setting program I introduced.

First, we discussed their overall dream in life. Then, during the sessions, employees learned how to break down their big vision into small, manageable chunks. That way they could celebrate little successes and weren't so likely to abandon their dream when they hit a rough patch.

We've all set big goals and then two weeks later, life got in the way or we got off track and we quit. In goal setting, I wanted to make it all easy to win and hard to lose.

Second, everyone learned to apply Doc Vik's "80/20 Rule": Stay on track 80 percent of the time; that way, you won't get discouraged or think about quitting if, for 20 percent of the time, you find you've veered off course. The goal-setting program was completely voluntary, and the goals could be work related or personal. (The three most common goals employees set concerned their career, weight loss, and personal financial management.)

There was one teammate who spent a lot of quality time sitting in the throne in my office. She was solution focused, and we would talk about all kinds of things that could and should be taken to the Next Level. She impressed me early by her focus, determination, and passion about empowering others. It didn't take long for others to notice her qualities also. Her name is Augusta Scott, and she's now the Life/Goals Coach at Zappos and is doing a terrific job. As she works on coaching programs, she also heads the speaking team at Zappos. Yep, she and I spent a lot of time together, and I miss her dearly, but I'm proud she is continuing to help take new generations of Zappos employees to the Next Level!

Give them your direct line

For my chiropractic practice, I had a coach I used to fly out to Arizona to see every month. For three years Dr. Fred and I would get together, and he would coach me through my practice challenges. On one of my visits, I said that I was sometimes inconvenienced by patients calling me at home at all hours of the day and night. There were times when someone would phone me at midnight because he was lying on the kitchen floor unable to move. More than once on a Saturday afternoon I'd hear from someone who had turned awkwardly and now couldn't move her neck without excruciating pain.

Since the best service and experience was what I was all about, I couldn't refuse to answer the phone, make a house call, or meet them at my office. What was I to do? Dr. Fred told me in his stern South African accent, "Give them your home number." I was floored! If I gave my home number to all of my thousands of patients, I would surely be answering the phone at odd hours even more.

"Trust me," Dr Fred said. "If they know that you have their back, no pun intended, they will leave you alone."

A funny thing happened. After I gave my home number to my patients, the off-hours calls stopped. Dr. Fred was right. When my patients knew they could call my home number anytime they had a problem, they stopped calling. They would come in during office hours more regularly, and, whenever they could, they wouldn't wait or put off situations until they became emergencies. When I told them, "I'm glad to see you are doing much better because you haven't called me in quite a while," the patients nearly all responded, "Oh, I still have occasional problems, but you were so nice to give me your home number, I didn't want to bother you. I know you care, and you will always be there for me, and I realized it could wait until normal business hours."

WHAT IF HE STAFF . . .

- Met with all the employees individually and just talked or listened to them get things off their chest?
- Gave employees a direct line and personal e-mail too? Employees probably won't use them—at least not often—but they'll feel a lot safer knowing that they have the option.

The results will be better relationships and a channel for open communication.

Here's a suggestion for a job description for a key player in your new Human Empowerment Department:

Job Title: Human Empowerment Coach

Vision/Purpose: Help employees reach their full potential

Summary Description: Empower employees

Tasks and Responsibilities: Training, leadership, communication and relationship building

Functions: Foster empowerment, teamwork, and unity

Supervisor/Advisor: Best-suited person in the HE department
Qualifications: People-oriented person with great energy and leadership abilities along with relationship and communication skills

Skills Necessary: Ability to inspire and motivate while maintaining the corporate Culture as the company grows

Experienced Desired: Trained Coach and or someone with experience empowering, inspiring, and motivating people; someone who thinks out of the box (perhaps a coach, retired coach, teacher, athlete); corporate background not a prerequisite

Working Hours: 3–5 days a week, or whatever will work for the current size or demands of your company

Create a can-do mind-set

HR—or the new HE—can help any company when staff aligns its programs with the Culture.

I've mentioned the saying I used at Zappos—"Spin it & Win it." This meant that *whenever you face a challenge, you "spin it" into a positive, an opportunity, or a lesson.* Everyone knew that phrase and used it often.

How about helping your employees with a "can-do" mind-set?

It had tremendous benefits for the employees' personal and professional lives.

Put positive signs around the company to guide the mind-set.

Remember, however, that positive signs can't counteract a negative Culture. If you are changing HR into HE or transforming your Culture to be more empowering, though, let the world know it. If everyone is aware that they are in transition, going from "what is" to "what will be," the new Culture will be adopted more easily.

Write a positive daily blog

That's what we did at Zappos with drvik.com. Daily motivational and inspirational messages were delivered to all employees over the company intranet every day except weekends and holidays. Give your employees the opportunity to start their day reading something positive.

Goal setting works wonders

We had great success with goal setting at Zappos, but after other companies took the cue from us, I heard that the process wasn't working so well for them. When I asked what they were doing, I heard, "We asked employees to make professional goals, and the success rate wasn't too good."

The reason was obvious: these companies didn't quite understand that if employees weren't doing well in their personal life, setting professional goals didn't matter. And even if they *were* doing well in their personal lives, the professional goals were seen as just pushing them to do more. So by only setting professional goals in your company and not wanting to empower your employees personally, what you are saying to them is, "Set bigger goals at work, so you can work more and work harder . . . for us."

Experiencing wins in one's personal life allows for more empowerment overall; work gets better, too—because newly empowered employees improve all aspects of their lives.

Set personal goals with your employees first, and if they want to set professional goals later, great. At least give them an option. Experiencing wins in one's personal life allows for more empowerment overall; work gets better, too—because newly empowered employees improve all aspects of their life.

Wouldn't you feel great if a company was personally empowering you, instead of driving you to do more at work? Your answer is most likely "Yes," because you know that if you are doing better personally, you will then do more professionally. But you also need to be patient.

Streamline hiring

What are your hiring practices? Is it one applicant at a time for a two-hour interview? Why not make the process fun and engaging for both applicants and employees?

Hold an open application meeting. Set aside a certain time of day when the applicants come in as part of a group. An employee should champion the meeting and let everyone know, in the group setting, about job details and expectations. After a brief summary—which always lets the applicants know about the company's Vision, Purpose, and Values—allow anyone to leave if the job is not for them. You can't be everything to everyone, and, usually, only a few people leave. As for the ones who stay, they'll know what your company does, why your company does it, and what you all value! Even if the company is not for them, they just may tell others who might want to join the organization.

Then, for the remaining candidates, set up interviews—three or five minutes apiece—with three of your employees. Use a set of prearranged questions, and have your employees rate the candidates. This type of hiring technique isn't perfect for all positions, but I did this at my clinic when we needed to hire a lot of new folks. Man, did it save time! It also helps you quickly see who rises to the top, and the really cool part is that it is fun for everyone.

Once the group interviews are completed, you can sort out the candidates you want to call back to make an offer or for further interviews.

The process empowers your employees, as they have a say in whom you hire and whom they will be working with.

You can also have more fun with your interview process and combine a few job duties with the interview. This may sound hokey—OK, it *is* hokey—but it works. In my clinic, back in the day when I was hiring for a receptionist or insurance department positions, we let the applicants know that the interview paid $5, and we also asked them to bring in a red apple. Why? Because we wanted people who would do what they were asked and who were not afraid to ask for money—prerequisites for those jobs. The ones who brought in the red apple and asked for the $5 after the interview usually got the job.

YOUR OWN COMPANY UNIVERSITY

Does your company have an internal training department, a "college" or "university" that helps employees move to the Next Level? Your HE department can provide benefits in the form of such classes, which help employees develop personally as well as professionally.

For example, you can have history classes to pass along the background and traditions of your company. How about Excel and word-processing classes to help them be better qualified? How about having a speed-reading class for personal empowerment? How about having an accounting class focused on budgeting and saving? Is there a goal-setting workshop?

We can always train someone to do a job or a task, but we can't always train someone to be nice. The Starbucks founder and CEO hires only people who smile.

There is no need to have all the classes focus on company matters; it's the people who count. When you empower your employees at a personal level, they will reciprocate and help move the company forward.

LOOK FOR A "CULTURE FIT"

Fitting into the Culture is the very reason we pay so much attention to the people we accept for employment. Applicants can be as smart as a whip, but if they are difficult to deal with, they don't fit the Culture and should be dismissed.

I had experienced this when I hired docs for the clinic. I brought on some "hot shot" docs early in my career, but I found that even though they knew their stuff, they didn't have a good bedside manner with patients, let alone with staff. For a service organization, we wanted people-oriented staff members, not experts with an attitude. And so we placed 50 percent of our emphasis on culture fit and the other 50 percent on aptitude. That way we could all work as a team to get things done. We could always help train our docs in facts and practices, but we couldn't train them to be nice.

Standout team members who can't get along end up spoiling the Culture of the team.

A lot of us have a favorite professional football team, and we have all heard about the player who thinks only of himself. That is a perfect example of someone's spoiling a team's Culture. Everywhere the selfish player goes, he ends up screaming—at his coach, quarterback, or other team members. Sure, these guys are great athletes. But a team is not made of just one player, and after a while there usually is a list of teams that don't want him. This player would have been a more powerful teammate if he fit into the Culture. A player who's only concerned about himself will end up . . . by himself.

The new HE delivers fun!

Since the new HE department creates great relationships, those staff members can be responsible for seeing that everyone has fun.

Breaking up the workday with fun times really helps improve the morale—almost as much as food does. Does your HE department have an ambassador of fun? Organizing children's and spouses' days and events promotes unity among those who give their days to your company.

CELEBRATIONS

HE should recognize that *celebrations* are a great way to increase the fun at work and break the monotony of redundant tasks. *Potlucks*, too, bring people together, increase communications, and solidify relationships.

Your HE department can arrange ice cream socials, cookouts, potlucks, and employee, vendor, and customer appreciation days. Oh, and don't forget a "we don't need a reason" approach to delivering food to your employees. Food creates good morale as well as good communication and helps cement long-lasting relationships.

COMMUNICATION

As we've said, communication—or lack thereof—is often the biggest challenge in a company, especially one that's growing. Don't let your teams or departments get "siloed" into isolation.

An "all hands on deck" meeting is a great way to get the company together, and if you don't have enough space to include everyone at the meeting, stream it live to the biggest rooms that will accommodate as many people as possible to hear the message.

There should be a "group takeaway" from the meeting, a common affirmation.

As far as I am concerned, almost everything that makes up a company's Culture can and should be championed by HE.

And as HE enhances positive feeling about working at your company, you'll find your customers benefit, too, as we'll see in the next part of the book.

This Is Essential to the Process—
Customers & Customer Service

The customer is always right!

Make my day!

If it weren't for customers supporting us as a company and a Culture, there would be no company or Culture to talk about. Let's never forget that. We owe our customers our very existence, so let's show them we are grateful every chance we get and with every experience we can give them.

Regrettably, Customer Service is becoming *wallpaper*. Companies use it as a safety net to address customers' problems, questions, or concerns after they've bought a product, service, or knowledge. But if you need great customer service to put out fires, it's often too late; some customers that go into or slip past the net and are hard to win back. You shouldn't need to repair, fix, or improve your customer service in the first place.

Why not think about customer service more proactively, by putting it—in the form of experience—*into* the product, service, or knowledge you sell. If everyone did that, there would be no need to have customer service, per se. If you sold electronics, you'd help your customer use your product. If you made the product so intuitive that the user didn't need an instruction manual, like Apple does, the customer wouldn't need help to figure it out. Customer service would be a moot point.

But customer service is a necessity when there's been neglect along the way. Because when you create customer service at the end of the experience, it's really just a complaint department.

You won't need to fix things if things don't break.

Customer service is helping your customer find help and resolve a problem or complaint; better still, it's making sure those things don't happen in the first place so that your customers can spend time talking with friends and family instead of talking to a customer service representative.

We should want to make a customers' day, week, year, or lifetime, not simply satisfy them. Satisfaction is not what it's cracked up to be, and it only lasts so long. Satisfaction is passive; it doesn't elicit any emotion, and therefore no emotional connection is made.

If we can reach and retain a positive emotional connection with our customers, we have the chance to keep them for a lifetime.

When we do the math, we don't really need many new customers if we are able to keep the ones we already have.

In the early '80s, I had a friend who went to film school in Los Angeles and then worked briefly at Disneyland. He told me that the park had as many people on staff at night as during the day, refurbishing the rides and making sure everything was working perfectly. They didn't wait for things to break —and risk their customers having a very poor or dangerous experience. They cleaned, repaired, and maintained the facilities and equipment before things got dirty or broken. I took his word for it, and applied his comments not only to my clinic but also to other companies I've worked with. One thing my friend said has stuck with me: "At Disneyland, we clean, clean windows because when we clean, clean windows, they never get dirty!" Wow, how's that for proactively taking care of the customers you have and creating the best experience for them?

THE COST OF ACQUIRING NEW CUSTOMERS

Most companies have measured the cost of acquiring a new customer. But few, if any, have calculated the cost of retaining the customers they already have.

We spend more acquiring customers than we do keeping them.

Companies sell their products, service, or knowledge by means of salespeople or affiliates, along with advertising and marketing, and even discounts to new customers (which only infuriate existing customers and drive up acquisition costs as well). The number of new customers divided by the cost of attracting them is the customer acquisition cost.

Customer acquisition costs can be anywhere from five dollars to many hundreds or more, depending on what you sell.

But often there's no comparable amount spent on retaining customers. Take a business call center, which is normally staffed with employees who are trained to say no and get you off the phone as quickly as possible. Call center staff often provide little or no help for customers. They're not empowered to solve problems, deliver a positive experience, or create a relationship that results in customer loyalty. That's because most companies view their call centers as costs; they should consider them investment centers—beautiful places where your employees can invest their time and effort in creating long-term relationships with your customers.

The phone is a great way to create loyal customers and reduce the new customer acquisition cost.

However, the scale is usually tipped in the wrong direction, pouring company resources into *acquiring* new customers rather than *retaining* them.

At the risk of sounding like a broken record, let me remind you that the same applies to your employees. Companies spend a lot on recruiting, interviewing, and hiring employees. Once the new folks are in the door, though, not as much time, energy, and money is dedicated to keeping them engaged or happy (which translates into loyalty). Think of that old song and treat your workers as if you "only have eyes" for them.

If we did everything we could to take care of the customers we have, that effort would pay for itself over and over again.

Look at it this way: If an average customer spends $200 a year and the lifetime of buying is 50 years, that person will spend $10,000 if you keep them happy. If your initial customer acquisition cost was $50, you will receive $9,950 in gross revenue from just that one customer. Actually, however, your list of new customers will grow with virtually no cost to the company because that one customer's word of mouth over the years will have a snowball effect on your income. Think of the revenue stream generated just by keeping this one customer happy. Then multiply that by the total number of your customers; you'll have all the business you can handle.

Conversely, when a company loses an existing customer as fast as it acquires a new one, income will never grow. It's as though you have a hole in your bucket: whatever you put in will drain out at the same rate, and the bucket will never fill. More often than not, unsatisfied customers usually tell their friends, and that drives the customer acquisition costs up. As it becomes increasingly difficult to acquire customers, the company's income plummets, along with its fate.

Best Buy: casualty of the Information Age

Back in 2007, as I started to travel more, I needed a laptop with access to the Internet to function properly as the Coach at Zappos. I went to Best Buy. I wanted a small, light laptop that handled basics, like e-mail. The salesperson showed me a model with many more features, and, not really knowing much about computers at that time, I agreed that I needed 10 times more speed and storage than my home computer had. Long story short, I purchased the beast.

My next trip was about six weeks away, so after about 30 days, I unpacked the new laptop and tried it out. (There hadn't been a floor model to demo at the store.) When I turned it on, I noticed the cursor was darting all over the page like a jumping flea, and when I wrote e-mail, many times the cursor would either erase the e-mail or send what I was writing before I was finished writing it. Becoming more and more frustrated, I took the laptop back to Best Buy to return or exchange it.

Initially, I was escorted to someone who tried to fix the problem right there. No such luck. He told me he had seen "a lot of these models do that," and I just had "to deal with it or send it back to the factory." And how long would I be without the laptop? "About six to eight weeks."

Of course the reason I had bought the laptop in the first place was because I needed it for travel, and I was leaving the following week. The employee also let me know that the factory probably wouldn't do anything to fix the problem, as it was a common occurrence with these models. Once again, he said, I would just have "to deal with it."

In that case I said I would like my money back. But since I was a little over the 30-day return deadline, there was nothing he could do. (If I had come in before the month was out, he might have been able to give me store credit—minus a restocking charge.) Well, then, could I exchange this $1,000 laptop for the one I originally wanted that was only $400 and get store credit for the difference? "No," he said. Well, what if I gave you the $1,000 laptop back, and got the $400 laptop, and we called it even? Once again the answer was "No," even though I was willing to leave $600 dollars on the table.

So I left Best Buy with a computer that I could not rely on to work properly and said to myself, This is ridiculous. Best Buy's service and return policies are *horrendous*, along with the customer's experience.

Fast-forward to 2012. I read an article in *Fortune* magazine by an author who witnessed "retail's present and future collide in a Best Buy. It was ugly." Turns out a 20-something couple was shopping for a flat-screen there. They fiddled with the dials; mauled the remotes, thumped the speakers, and researched models to their hearts' delight. When they settled on a particular Samsung LED, the guy whipped out his phone, captured a QR code on the TV, and beamed it up to the Web to check for more favorable prices.

"It's 49 bucks cheaper through Amazon," he said to his girlfriend.

They rubbed salt into Best Buy's wound by ordering the TV while still standing in the store, enjoying Best Buy's endless display of models, to the benefit of Amazon—and themselves, of course.

One month later, after first-quarter results came in, I read these headlines on the Internet: "Best Buy Going Down" and "Best Buy Implodes." The subtitle added "Best Buy to close 50 stores."

Reading further, I learned that Best Buy's plans to turn around the company included enhancing the customer experience and lowering prices. Hopefully a better return policy will be part of that new customer experience.

Of course, if Best Buy had been delivering a better experience all along, then it wouldn't have had to also lower prices. It should have kept to what the store's name implied: give its customers the "best buy," which includes treating them like they matter.

Not just a buzzword

For most companies, customer service has not caught up with the times. Customer service used to take place in person, then it was over the phone, and now it relies on the phone, Internet, and various other devices. The connection that worked in the past has not caught up with the new way of providing customer service. How can we get back the personal touch in customer service? How can we create a better experience for the customer? By weaving it into the experience instead of leaving it to the end.

Back in the day, every gas station was a service station. As a kid, I remember my dad driving into a Texaco, say, and the attendant would fill up the car with gas, wash the windows, put air in the tires, and check the oil. The attendant would not watch you tend to your car and then provide "customer service" at the end by asking, Was your visit OK and is there anything I can do to help, oh, and can you go online and fill out a survey? Remember to put in my name—it's Bob.

How can we get back the personal touch in customer service?

Customer service at the old gas stations was woven into your visit and not just some baloney tacked on at the end. My father and I always felt like we were taken care of, that we mattered to the company selling us their gas.

Today, at a gas station, you are on your own. No attendant, no window washing, no attention to your tires, water, or oil. If you want these services, you need an appointment. Except that my wife has proved that statement wrong.

You see, every Wednesday she fills her car with gas at a 76 gas station near our house, because Wednesday is Ladies' Day, and the attendants pump the gas for you, and check the fluid levels and tire pressure. It's not the service station of the past, but on Wednesdays, if you are a lady, you don't have to get out of the car. My wife has never gotten too excited about pumping her own gas, so she started going to this station, and she loved it. She even planned her trips to make sure not to get close to empty before Wednesday. She shared the news with her friends, and they have told their friends. The place is doing a great business by word of mouth.

When my wife told me about this new gem of a business, I was impressed. She knew I needed to fix a back brake light and get an oil change, so she had asked the owner if they did that, and they did. She handed me his card and sent me on my way.

Oh, right, I thought, an oil change at a gas station; I'd probably get ripped off. But the place was so close to our house I thought I'd give it a try. If it didn't work out, I could blame my wife. (I'm joking . . .)

And I wanted to see what the station's commitment to service was like, so I tested it out. I stopped by without notice one morning after I dropped off my youngest at school, to see if they could take me. Absolutely, they said. I left my car and let them know that I needed it by one that afternoon. Would they call me when the car was ready? Then I walked home.

They called me two hours earlier than promised and let me know I could come by and pick up the car anytime I wanted. When I got there, a nice young lady handed me the bill. I was ready to see an overinflated price, so I prepared myself mentally, calculating, "oil change, new filter, replace back brake light. I'm looking at a couple hundred dollars." To my utter surprise, the bill read $59.00. Just $59.00 for everything? Unbelievable. They had even replaced my brake light for the price of the bulb—$4.25. I was so excited, I told them that from then on I would bring my car there for everything and would also tell my friends.

How can we create a better experience for the customer?

I drove away happy as I could be with a new business that treated me like I matter.

That was Friday. On Monday, my phone rang, and it was a local number I didn't recognize. "Hi, this is Eddie from the 76 station that serviced your car on Friday."

"Yeah?" I said.

"Just wanted to let you know that we appreciate your business, and if you ever need us for anything in the future, please don't hesitate to call us or stop by."

"OK, Eddie, and I appreciate how your business treats people. As a matter of fact, I can't wait to tell others!"

"Thanks so much. You have a great week, OK?"

After I hung up, I was nearly in shock. I had been waiting for the other shoe to drop, to have Eddie ask me to do a survey, go to a website to answer some stupid self-serving questions, or find out how I could win a vacation for two in Jamaica if I filled out a questionnaire online. Nope, Eddie asked for nothing. Zero. Nada. He just thanked me.

Wow! How simple. I wish other businesses would start doing this, don't you?

What's really important in all this is that in the past, people usually told a few friends about a good or bad experience, but today, with the Internet and social media, word of a good or bad experience can reach millions. And a bad experience typically travels a lot farther and faster than good news.

We can advertise whatever we want, but social media have their own voice and opinion.

With the speed of social media, negative comments can take a company down in an instant. Mark Twain isn't around in the Information Age, but even in his time, some things moved pretty quickly:

"A lie runs around the earth when the truth is just putting on its shoes."—Mark Twain

Certainty is something you can count on

As you read further, you'll see that customers may say they want things like value, service, low price, high quality, selection, guarantees, and so on, but one thing they all agree on is that they want "certainty." We need to be consistent with our product, service, knowledge, and delivery. And, once again, this all starts with providing your employees with the certainty that you've got their best interests—as people, not pawns—at the top of your mind.

CUSTOMERS ASK, "DO YOU HAVE . . . ? CAN YOU GET . . . ?"

Great customer service should always come down to saying "Yes" instead of "No," but that's not always the case. Brad, my friend who owns Restaurant Equipment World, sells first-aid kits in the Middle East. Why? Because his customers asked for them. Though his business is restaurant supply, he provides the kits simply because they asked him to do so.

He also told me about an account he won by delivering a 58-cent item that no one else would deliver. This company needed a 58-cent part that no other person or company would sell because they wouldn't make any money on it; it would actually have cost more than the company could make off the sale. Brad didn't care; he was all about saying "Yes" when his customers asked him for something. The customer had asked him for it and he delivered it, no question. That 58-cent item resulted in future orders totaling more than a million dollars.

Talk about customer service and then some!

So, what are you giving up when you say "No"?

Are you listening to customers when they say, "Do you have . . . ? Can you get . . . ?"

GOING THE EXTRA MILE

We've all heard this saying before, so why do so few companies practice it? Take a good look at the restaurants in your town. Which ones have a line out the door? Probably only a few, if any. Where I live, there are only a couple of dining spots—less than 1 percent of the total—where patrons actually line up to get a table.

And why is there a line out the door? Because the place is providing a service, and, most likely, great customer service that meets the desires, needs, and demands of its customers. It could be a totally unique experience or food that you can't get anywhere else. It could be that the value is beyond compare. It could be that they give you more food than other restaurants. It could be a combination of things, but they're things the customers want, need, or demand, and the restaurant is delivering them like no other.

That 1 percent of restaurants knows what it takes to stand out.

ONE BUCK ALLOWED MY FRIEND TO "RETIRE"

A friend of mine owned a Mexican restaurant and told me that on his biggest plate, which sold for $12, the food cost was less than $2. He did a nice business but had to advertise to get his customers, and the ones who came in, didn't always come back. He was in a cycle of marketing and advertising to keep his restaurant half full, and the marketing and advertising costs were not cheap.

Eventually he decided that enough was enough; he wanted to stop the marketing expenses, which were a drain on his budget. So what did he do? Instead of spending $2 for his ingredients, he upped it to $3.

What happened? His customers got more for their money and no longer felt gypped by their regular meal. Instead they were treated to a WOW experience. After a while, customers were lining up out the door—without the cost of advertising. My friend was now making money hand over fist, and the customers not only came, they returned. He opened six more restaurants and now spends most of his time on vacation.

Why do so few restaurants attract customers in this way? Because they are the ones that truly go the extra mile. Their customers appreciate the gesture, and they say so by coming back again and again.

Incredible isn't it? Only a few restaurants really get what it means to go the extra mile. Why? Perhaps those that do have asked themselves these questions—just as you should do periodically with your team:

- How are we treating our customers?
- If we were our own customer, would we want to eat or shop somewhere else?
- What are we doing to take care of the customers we have?
- Is the call center for our business viewed as an expense or an investment?
- Are we training your representatives to say yes or no?
- Is our website up to date and easy to use?
- Do we treat our customers like our best friends?
- Are we "buffing out" our regular and new customers alike?

A customer service gem from Zappos

This is a beautiful example of customer service that wows. If Zappos doesn't carry what the customer wants, representatives are encouraged to research up to five other companies (online or in a shop near where the customer lives) to locate the product the customer is looking for. If the representative finds the item, he or she will let the customer know where to purchase the item.

I've done it myself. In 2005, when I went through Zappos' customer service training, I searched other stores to find an item a customer was looking for. The customer couldn't believe it when I told him where he could find what he wanted in his size, style, and color. "Why would you send me to your competition?" he asked. I replied, "Who will you come back to?" There was a short pause and then he whispered a drawn-out reply, "Riiiiggggghhhht."

> *We must treat our customers like our best friends.*

In the restaurant business, repeat customers are called regulars. The staff knows what these customers want and anticipates their needs. Regulars get the royal treatment and are treated like they really matter, and in return they're incredibly loyal. Having enthusiastic fans of your business is worth its weight in gold, because they will share with others the fabulous experiences they have.

Customers vote with their wallets. Remember what I asked you in the section about Unique/WOW Factors? Are you in the selling business or the reorder business? Is your marketing budget too high because you are trying to sell to new customers instead of taking care of the customers you already have?

You may have heard about that famous radio station, WIIFM—What's

In It For Me? Your customers are dialed in to it, so you need to deliver not only your product but also what's in it for them. You need to think hard about how to win their business for life. That way, you won't be in the selling business, you'll be in the reorder business.

Not too long ago I went to a two-day golf retreat. With just ten people in the group, we got to know each other pretty well. Two of the attendees were some of the very first employees at one of the top three online stock brokerage companies that have displaced most retail stockbrokers. One of them was responsible for all of the firm's branches across America. I asked her what differentiated the company from its two big rivals. Her answer was "great customer service." And she was responsible for making sure all the branches were delivering it.

Whatever you give, you will get in return. It works!

She would visit the branches and ensure that when someone walked through the door, employees would get up and greet them with respect. Yet, when I let her know that I was with Schwab and that they have great customer service, too, she nodded. "I know, we all do," she said.

What I was looking for when investing, I told her, was the ability to know when big investors and institutions bought or sold a particular stock. At present, I have to pay a private company for that service. When would her company offering something like that? She said they were working on upgrading their sites and systems, but what I was describing was still a couple of years away. Their emphasis now, she repeated, was great customer service.

What struck me then was that there was no real difference among the three big players. They all have great customer service, but it is not woven into the brokerage sites themselves, and not much separates one site from another. No wonder many folks don't really care who their online broker is. They go for the one who can give them the cheapest price on buying and selling stock.

Loyalty begins with you thinking of them

You want to attract customers, right? Put yourself into these two scenarios.

SCENARIO 1

Focus only on yourself. First, put on some nice, expensive clothes, just to make sure everyone notices you. The ones who can't afford what you wear will feel bad about themselves, so then you can feel good about you. Primp in the bathroom and fuss with your hair. Then ask everyone you see, "How does my hair look?" and "Don't I look nice?"

When you get to work, you can ask (as you always do) someone to help you with your work, or better yet, to do your work for you.

When you get home, take over the house and watch your TV programs. The spouse and kids can wait on you hand and foot. Why not? You deserve it.

Listen, you may think you deserve it, but when you don't give anything to anyone else, no one wants to give anything back. Your friends will get sick of telling you how nice you look. Your coworkers will find it hard to do your work. Your spouse will be turned off, and your kids will be hiding. So if you want to attract customers—or anyone else—maybe you should stop thinking of you.

SCENARIO 2

You wake up and tell your family you love them. You dress in whatever will not burden your family financially. When you leave the house, you pick up your neighbor's paper and put it on his front doorstep.

When you get to work, you say hello to everyone and perhaps exchange some high fives. Pass out a few compliments. Everyone knows that they can come to you for help or anything else they need. You work in an unbelievable environment where everyone is helpful and kind. During your work week you get a lot done, and you can't wait to see your coworkers every Monday.

When you arrive back home, you give everyone a big hug and ask them about their day. When you hear about your loved ones' experiences, you couldn't be happier. Your family loves you, and you love them.

Now translate these scenarios to your customers. You can easily see which circumstances will attract them and keep them happy. A friend of mine, Mark Sanborn, wrote a book called *The Fred Factor*, which highlights the value in thinking of and helping others. I highly recommend this book. Trust the process; it works.

Companies have to quit focusing on themselves and only "taking." They have to start "giving" for a change —and to fully understand what it means to say:

Whatever you give will come back to you.

The relationship you have with your customers will determine how they see you and what they say you are. That's your brand, and it's the subject of the next section.

This Is What They Say About Us— Brand

Brand:

The identity of a specific product, service or business.

Ask external and internal customers who they think you are

OK, if you have created, aligned, articulated, and implemented everything in the book so far, what you want people to say about you will be what they say about you. That will be your brand. If they aren't saying what you want to hear, you need to look back over your Vision, Purpose, Business Model, Unique/WOW Factors, Values, and Culture to see where you have gone astray.

Let me repeat that. A brand is mostly the end result of any company's Vision, Purpose, Business Model, Unique/WOW Factors, Values, and Culture—which are all a part of what you sell. A brand can take many forms, including a name, sign, symbol, color combination, or slogan. And a legally protected brand name is called a trademark. Brand has evolved to encompass identity—in effect, the personality of a product, company, or service.

> A brand is what *customers* say about you, not what *you* say about you.

So, what are you doing to influence customers' comments? Have you aligned your Vision, Purpose, Business Model, Unique/WOW Factors, Values, and Culture into something that will result in a powerful or positive brand?

A key to business is a good reputation. That's basically what a brand is; it's what you are known for. If you have a poor return policy, then that is what you will be known for. If you are a restaurant with a signature dish, that is what you are known for. A brand is what you sell and/or deliver to the customers and is usually tied to your Unique/WOW Factors.

The shortcut to finding out your company's brand is to ask these questions:

- What do your customers say about you?

- What do they think of your company?

- What do your customers say you are?

The answers to those questions will let you know if you are on track.

You have to commit to this process and really pay attention to what people say. If it's the voice of the majority, listen!

I bet we all know someone who is so full of himself that it's not funny, yet everyone knows it but him. Regretfully, many companies are the same as that person. The only way you will get the truth is to let go of your ego. Sure, you run the risk of hearing the equivalent of "Your baby is ugly." But that's exactly the kind of information you need to know. Whatever you hear about your company, take note, because it offers an opportunity to become better.

A brand comes from your customers

The owner of a Georgia barbecue pit had a sign saying "Best Barbecue in Georgia." When asked if it was true, he responded, "That's what people tell us." The brand was propagated by word of mouth, saving on advertising and marketing expenses. People's beliefs about you can be priceless.

Don't forget to ask your internal customers—your employees—too!

The brand inside your company creates the brand outside it.

Branding nuts

Here's an example of how one company in the nut-growing industry helped brand its product—and created a positive emotional experience with at least one customer.

This particular pistachio grower understood it needed to separate itself from the rest of the "nut family" in order to increase sales and customer loyalty. It created advertisements that touted the nuts' value. The idea was to attract customers by allowing them to easily repeat a message, which could turn into what the customers said about them—becoming the brand.

This was the entire commercial:

The Pistachio Nut

Lowest Calorie Nut

Lowest Fat Nut

That was it—easy to understand and easy to repeat. It convinced me that the pistachio nut is the best nut to eat. I instantly identified with their brand. Apparently, so did others. The message worked so well, in fact, that the company distilled the brand more and gave it an action step, so that the message evolved to:

Lowest Fat Nut

Heart Healthy

Get Crackin'

I always knew nuts were good for me, but I was concerned with calories and fat content, and I never really knew which nut was the best when it came to those things. My new understanding will now drive me toward buying pistachio nuts. And since the message of the commercial is easy to remember and repeat, I can let my friends know as well. It's great word of mouth. Branding genius!

A great brand creates an emotional connection.

Here are some additional examples of what companies have done to create their brand as well as give their customers feel-good emotional connections.

APPLE

Apple did it right. When someone wants to be hip and cool, they look hip and act cool. They avoid doing things that make them look inept or feel that way. So what does that mean for Apple products? The company aligned its Vision, Purpose, Business Model, Unique/WOW Factors, and Values and emerged with the brand it wanted. Their products not only look hip and cool but also stand out from the rest with sleek lines, thin silhouettes, and even just a single cord as opposed to the many of other desktop computers. Check out the packaging for Apple products, too. The materials and designs are works of art, projecting the same image as Apple products: hip, cool, and sleek.

Apple does one more thing that allows you to look hip and cool. It makes them easy to use. Never use an iPhone? No problem, it's intuitive. You can't really make a mistake putting a new name in the directory; you are guided through it. Heck, even *I* feel hip and cool when someone asks me to put their contact information in my phone; it's easy as pie. It was a very different experience when someone asked me to do the same thing with my old BlackBerry. I couldn't do it and I felt like a moron. I am not too tech savvy, and BlackBerry didn't help me out. Some of my friends would even laugh at me for not being able to add a contact to my phone; they had to do it for me.

VIRGIN GROUP

It seems like all the Virgin companies take on the persona of founder Sir Richard Branson. With his movie star looks and flowing locks, he has to be one of the hippest guys in the world. They should put his picture next to the definition of "cool" in the dictionary. His attitude has gone into the DNA of all Virgin products.

Ever take a Virgin Atlantic flight? The seats, the TVs, the interior, the color, the lighting—everything is stylish and up-to-date. Getting on or off a Virgin plane, I feel as though I'm royalty.

And Virgin is a far cry from most other airlines I have flown on. With baggage fees, poor service, and uninspired décor, all other carriers are commodities; nothing differentiates one from the rest. I feel cheap waiting, flying, and deplaning because of the way they treat me—like a nobody. And making me feel cheap is not the path to a favorable experience.

But there is one exception—Southwest, which treats its customers like they matter. Southwest planes leave the gates on time and arrive on time or even early. I fly a lot and have never been late on a Southwest flight.

So even though I may not feel like a high roller when I fly Southwest, I do feel like royalty when I look at all the flight status boards in the airline terminals and see nothing but canceled or delayed flights for other airlines. Southwest's brand? Nice people who get you there on time. Southwest treats you like you matter.

How to develop your brand

Ironically, your brand is the last thing you should attempt to determine, because it is the result of everything else you have been doing. You can't just create a brand, nor can you create a reputation. Both are built over time by what you do and how you do it.

With a company, you need to start everything with your employees. How you treat them will be reflected in your brand.

A brand is developed by what you do and how you do it. Starting the process with the employees is usually the best plan.

Let's look at it this way: If you want your customers to brand your company as one with great service, but you treat your employees badly, do you really believe that your employees will deliver great service? Maybe, but that will last for only a short time because employees who are treated poorly will eventually treat the customers the same way they are treated. No one can mistreat us and expect a loving hug and smile in return. Whatever you want out of your brand, you've got to put it into your employees first. Think about what you want your customers to brand you as and work backward from there.

GIVE YOUR EMPLOYEES GREAT EXPERIENCES, AND THEY WILL PRODUCE THEM FOR OTHERS

If you want your brand to be about experience, for instance, your workplace shouldn't be an uninspiring bland building with white paint on every wall.

Imagine that you have a tea company whose brand is to deliver the finest and best-tasting teas to the world, but all your employees hate the taste of tea. Do you think they will talk enthusiastically about your product? Will they bother to learn the subtle differences in taste among the teas? Do you think they will be able to describe and market the teas to the folks who want the best-tasting brews? No, no, and no.

Whatever you want your brand to become, have your employees live and breathe it first.

YOUR BRAND IS YOUR IDENTITY AND YOUR REPUTATION

Make sure everyone in your company regards your brand highly and is committed to protecting it. You can say your brand is "Excellence." But if your products are inferior and your service is even worse, no matter what you say you are, customers will send word out through cyberspace that your brand is "Sucky." You'll never recover from that bad press. But if your employees are motivated to protect your brand, they would do everything in their power to rectify the product or the service and get things back on track. If your employees weren't passionate about what you sold or delivered and didn't live and breathe your brand, they probably wouldn't care what was shipped out to customers.

KEEP YOUR BRAND MESSAGE SHORT AND SWEET

Just as the Vision, Purpose, and Values need to be short and clear, you need to create concise and repeatable messaging for your brand or what you want your brand to be.

Pick a couple of words, a saying, or an experience that you want your customers to remember and repeat. This would become your brand.

Initially, Zappos' was "WOW!" We did everything we could to deliver WOW! first from our employees and then from our customers. Then all of the folks who visited Zappos looked around and said WOW! Pretty simple: easy to remember and repeat and different from any other brand I know of. Nice work, Zappos.

Is your brand trustworthy?

A brand allows the customer to know what to expect. We can market our brand to look good in brochures, but if what is delivered doesn't live up to the hype, we won't be around for long. Ultimately, a brand is what *the customer experiences.*

A brand also needs to elicit *predictability* and *repeatability.* Customers need to know what they can expect anytime they choose to interact with your company.

Processes and procedures are necessary to create consistency in brand. McDonald's regulates its processes to ensure that each customer gets the same hamburger anywhere in the world. A McDonald's cheeseburger in Los Angeles tastes the same as a cheeseburger in Detroit or even in Copenhagen, Denmark. Every cheeseburger is made exactly the same. The attention to process creates a consistent final product.

Once a brand has dominance in the marketplace, it can use that power to promote other aspects of the business.

A predictable, reliable, and dominant brand can capitalize on its name to increase pricing. Take a look at the products you keep coming back to. Some of them probably aren't the least expensive products in their space. Most of us buy some well-known brands that cost more because they align with what we want, need, or demand. For that kind of fit and consistency, we don't mind paying a bit more.

Brands change with the times, and products evolve with customer demands

Today four out of the five top-selling beer brands are "light" beer. In the 1960s, though, when a light beer was introduced, it quickly failed, because it was before its time. That's an example of how brands have evolved through the changing wants, demands, or needs of its customers.

Remember the discussion of Sears' Craftsman tools as a Unique/WOW Factor? That was what the company was known for, and it was part of its brand. But as the Unique/WOW Factor of offering quality and dependable tools faded, that affected the company, too.

People want what they want.

Coca-Cola is one of the biggest and most trusted brands in the world. People love the consistency and refreshing nature of the beverage. In 1985, though, the company changed its formula from Original Coke to New Coke, and the backlash was so intense that the formula had to be changed back. Consumers want what they want.

Aligning your brand with the wants and demands of your customer is key.

In a *Consumer Reports* survey of Car Brand Perception, the magazine detailed how consumers scored a car in the following categories: Safety, Quality, Value, Performance, Design/Style, Technology/Innovation, and Environmentally Friendly/Green. Today's consumer is looking at all these qualities when buying a car, so an automobile company needs to align its Vision, Purpose, Business Model, Unique/WOW Factors, and Values with those categories to achieve its desired outcome. Otherwise, it won't reflect the current wants, needs, and demands of its customers and sales will suffer.

Miscellaneous truths about brand

After a good deal of research and many experiences with clients on brands, I've come up with some thoughts about their hows, whys, and wherefores. Here are some ideas to consider as you create or polish your company's brand.

Great service is one of the best branding options for companies to deliver in the Information Age.

But why stop there? Why not live your brand with your vendors? While most companies only think of providing great service to their customers, it's the vendors who provide what you need to sell. And if you can buff out your vendors, over time it will be much easier to work with them as trusted partners to deliver your product, service, or knowledge.

Your customers will let you know that you are on point with what you say your brand is.

Alignment is key.

If you have a watch company and want your brand to be "The Finest Watches Made," you need to start with Vision, Purpose, Values, and Culture. When they are in place, all thoughts, decisions, and actions will be in alignment with your brand, and it will become what you wanted it to become—"the finest watches made."

This Is the Pot of Gold If We Do It Right—Experience & the Emotional Connection

---

It's the experience you give someone that they will always remember . . . if we make the experience great.

It's all about the experience

This is the place where everything should all come together—the reason why we have created the Culture and why our people bring it to life. Because beyond everything we have talked about, it's the experience that matters most.

Whatever happens in our daily lives, the end result is our experience. So what are we doing or what do we need to do to create the best experience for our employees, customers, vendors, and investors on a consistent basis?

If all the key aspects of our company have been aligned to produce a phenomenal experience, we have done the best job possible. We have secured the future of our company and of our jobs. We will have created a reorder business where our customers don't want to leave us. And the employees won't want to leave either.

HERE'S THE DEAL

A regular experience that merely satisfies—a so-so experience—doesn't elicit any kind of emotion. On the other hand, great or horrible experiences, those that get us excited or upset, do spark an emotion and will create an emotional connection (though, obviously, one emotion will be much more positive than the other).

There's a limit to how much we can control. Basically, we can direct the customers' experience up to their emotional reaction. After that, thanks to word of mouth and today's speed of communication, our repeat business is up to the customers. So we better make their experience great!

Start with our everyday actions to see if they are creating a so-so experience or a great one. Do we say "Hello" in the morning or do we grunt?

Do we say "Thank you" as often as we should or do we just take things for granted? Do we ask others how they are doing or do we just talk about ourselves? Do we convey the feeling that "I am too busy" or "I am never too busy"?

When we look around at the bounty or lack of it in our lives, there is a direct correlation between the experiences we create—good or not—and the fulfillment in our lives.

Why is it all about the experience?

We are attracted to things or repelled by them, depending on our past experiences.

Experiences that elicit emotions actually help us form memories. Why? It's how our brains work; it's how we are wired. The area that is responsible for the formation and storing of memories from emotional events is located in the limbic system, in a place called the amygdala.

But it's the really great or really bad experiences that create emotional reactions. There's no spark for so-so, merely good, or satisfactory experiences or expected events. And memories are not necessarily formed by a single emotional event; they can be, but they are usually patterned or conditioned in the brain over time. We may be conditioned to be fearful (fear conditioning) because of experiences that brought us harm, for instance. Positive (appetitive) conditioning results from experiences that were positive, that made us feel good, or that were good for us.

There is no spark for ordinary or expected events or experiences.

There is also a direct link through the amygdala to our sympathetic and parasympathetic nervous system. After conditioning from repeated emotional stimuli, we usually react to certain experiences reflexively or subconsciously.

The linking of our experiences with emotion and memory has helped us to evolve as a species to where we are today. We migrate toward experiences that have been good for us and stay away from those that have been bad.

We've all heard the expression, "Every generation needs to learn that the oven is hot." We burn ourselves once, and ouch! We have an emotional reaction and form an emotional connection to stay away from hot stoves, thanks to the memory that is created in the process. So for the rest of our lives, we avoid touching a hot stove. If we even get too near a hot burner, our reflexes take over, pulling us away from harm. We don't have to think about it.

Flip the coin over: When we experience something great, our autonomic nervous system takes over, and we reflexively want more of the same, so we keep going back to the experiences that were great. That keeps us safe and moving toward what has been good for us in the past.

A great experience creates an emotional reaction that forms an emotional connection and finally a memory that keeps attracting us to that great experience.

No matter whether it's a great or bad experience, an emotional reaction will turn into an emotional connection, especially if is repeated. After that, what happens, happens automatically. Our brains are programmed to remember and to make our reactions reflexive. From then on we are attracted or repelled without consciously thinking about it.

When it comes to our customers, every time we deliver a great experience and create an emotional reaction, *that* turns into an emotional connection. And customers program, pattern, or condition themselves to return. It may sound a bit contrived, like we are programming or manipulating people by the experiences we deliver, but we're not. We're just delivering experiences that, hopefully, they like a lot, and if that helps them come back to get more of what they like, all the better. It's a win–win situation.

We've seen it with Zappos. By first delivering WOW and now delivering happiness—a wonderful experience—the company has created long-term relationships with its customers and sees 75 percent return customers on any given day.

BROKEN RELATIONSHIPS

Relationships are broken for the following reasons:

1 percent die

5 percent move away

10 percent find someone new

17 percent communicate less and less

but

67 percent of relationships are broken because of one word: *indifference.*

Treat employees and customers like they don't matter, treat them like they are a number, treat them like you don't care about them—in essence, put indifference into the experience you deliver—and you will be alone in short order.

What should be the biggest thing your company is doing? The answer is obvious: Deliver the best experience in everything you do for employees and your customers alike. The results will be high percentages of repeat customers and low employee turnover.

You can achieve this if you follow the steps in this book.

Sometimes we don't remember why we dislike or avoid someone or something. We've simply forgotten what started our negative emotional connection, but we're still programmed to follow it. It's like the old feud between the Hatfields and McCoys. It's been going on for ages, though no one can remember how it started.

Emotional connections seem to last forever, and some continue for a lifetime, so keep that in mind the next time you think about increasing your profit margin by decreasing quality or customer service. People remember . . . and their attitude is this: "If you screw us (or even think about it), this time *you* are the party that is going down."

When Netflix raised prices with no conceivable added value, the customers fled in droves, and the stock price dropped substantially.

When Bank of America tried to charge a $5 fee for using the ATM, it created such an uproar that within days, the bank reversed the policy.

When Verizon tried to charge its customers a $2 fee for online bill payments, the reaction was swift, and the decision was rescinded within 24 hours.

COMPANIES: You can't add a fee without adding value, because your customers will react strongly and negatively, and they'll remember long after you forget.

WHAT IS THE LAST EXPERIENCE?

Usually the last thing the customer experiences is what heavily "colors" a customer's memory. What happens at the end is so important that you should not only focus on the overall experience but also pay close attention to the last part of the experience.

Imagine you're at a baseball game and enjoying every play, when, at the bottom of the ninth inning, your team's player hits the winning home run. As the ball sails out, the fan in front of you jumps up and spills a soda on you; it ruins the whole experience. Yet if the same person had spilled a soda over you in the first inning, but your team still hit the game-winning run, you'd come away feeling great about the win and probably wouldn't be thinking about the sticky soda on your clothes. We color our memory of an event with what we experienced last. So we must take great care with what happens at the end of any transaction.

You have won the game if your customers say, "I love giving them my business, because they treat me so well."

If you are doing anything to compromise the customer's experience—especially in the final part of the buying cycle or after—you will color that person's memory of the whole process adversely, and that's one of the worst things you can do as a business.

So what is the last thing your customers receive from you . . . a bill? Do they end up dealing with customer service because they have a question or concern? Do they have to fill out a survey? Or do they get a thank-you note? It's up to you and the experience you want to create, especially at the end.

What "color" are your customer's experiences?

The locomotion of emotional connection

At one time or another we all have felt an emotional connection with a product, service, or experience. Perhaps when we are watching TV, we see a commercial for a company that we are emotionally connected to. When that commercial airs, we may have said to ourselves, "Hey, I use them," or "That's the company I like," or even the ultimate, "I *love* that company and won't go to anyone else." When this happens, that company has done the right things; you may want to look at the things that company did and do them too.

SAVING TEN CENTS

I was doing some work for a company located a block away from AT&T Park, the new Giants Stadium, in San Francisco. I enjoyed going to work and liked the location, above a Safeway (my personal pantry) and next to a Wells Fargo Bank branch (my personal piggybank).

One day just before lunch, I suddenly got hungry for a nice, big tuna fish sandwich, on soft wheat bread with a little lettuce for crunch. I remembered that a coffee shop right behind the office had salads and sandwiches too, and I'd seen tuna listed on the giant blackboard behind the counter.

It wasn't exactly cheap—$7.95—but it sounded terrific; it even came with a salad dressed with vinaigrette. I anticipated the best tuna fish sandwich imaginable. Why not? I had always experienced great service in the coffee shop and I liked its indoor and outdoor seating areas.

After a short wait, a server delivered my meal. It looked all right, though both the salad and the sandwich seemed a bit small. That was OK.

I wanted a healthy meal, and I didn't want to overeat. I picked up half of the sandwich and took my first bite.

What was my experience? I chomped down on a hard crust of bread, and the force of my bite squeezed all of the tuna fish salad out onto my plate. When I took a closer look, I realized the sandwich had been prepared with the heel on the bottom and a softer slice facing up. A heel? That's the piece I always throw out for the birds. This is what I get for my $7.95?

(Side note: My father was a police officer for 25 years, and with just one income in the family, money was always tight. We watched every penny, and since I was the only boy between two sisters, I often got the heel as part of my sandwich, sometimes both heels. You can imagine how I feel about bread heels at this stage of my life.)

Now, a loaf of bread for a restaurant is around two bucks max, and with 20 slices per loaf, that's around 10 cents apiece. Whoever made my sandwich thought it was OK to ruin my experience to save 10 cents. That dime represents approximately 1 percent of the $7.95 price, but it was half of the sandwich. Poor decision.

The end result for me? I had an experience that created an emotional reaction, which turned into emotional connection that was not good at all. The coffee shop saved ten cents, but I will never order food there again. Why? They served me a heel, and I felt like a heel: ripped off, like I didn't matter.

A ten-cent decision eliminated my future business, and that of all of the people I have told.

Think about your company. Are you saving a dime but ruining your customer's experience?

I started out hating computers

My first experience with a computer was in 1974. I grew up in the Silicon Valley, and computers were the next big thing, so in my sophomore year in high school, I decided to choose a computer class for an elective. It covered FORTRAN or COBOL, or maybe both . . . it was a long time ago. The first day of class, I walked in and there was a machine the size of a bank vault taking up a good part of the classroom.

The teacher explained that we would work all quarter to produce a hundred or so punched-out computer cards that would create a program to print out the words "thank you." Are you kidding me? Work all quarter for that?

I toiled and toiled, with no idea of what I was doing, so I joined a study group with some football buddies, who knew less about computers than I did. We weren't having much success. When the teacher told us that the cards had to be in perfect order for the computer to read them, that explained a lot; we frequently dropped the stack of cards, and though we tried to get them in order, it was like trying to arrange random rocks.

Needless to say, I got a D in the class, the only D I ever received in high school, and for an elective, too! I decided then and there that computers were not going to be in my life anytime soon. That poor first taste of computers has led to a longstanding emotional connection—an aversion to computers.

Now I love computers . . . kind of

Fast-forward to when I had my clinic. I wanted to print a newsletter for my patients to better deliver information. My sister gave me her old Macintosh computer, and I slowly learned how to use it.

Even though I still had a distaste for computers, I really wanted the newsletter, so I started to write. I even learned to make columns to give it a newspaper look and feel.

After two weeks my newsletter was done, and I was ecstatic. All I had to do was to copy the file onto a 3-inch square of plastic and give it to the printer.

I was so excited that before I copied it, I got up to do a "happy dance" and when I did, I tripped the plug that went into the electrical outlet and pulled it out of the wall. My newsletter was gone!

I didn't know about the save button. Everything was lost. Two weeks of work down the tubes. I was devastated, frustrated, and, finally, angry. Once again, it was, "no more computers for me." This newsletter experience had reinforced my computer aversion.

I hate computers

Even though I didn't use computers myself, by the 1980s they were becoming important to every business. I installed them in my clinic and had them networked so everyone on the staff could work with them and communicate with the insurance department. In those days, almost everyone used IBM computers, which relied on certain keystrokes to implement commands. You had to use a computer language with colons and semicolons. Who had time or the motivation to remember that? Plus anything that required a colon and semicolon just wasn't for me.

When my friends said I should learn to use a computer, my response was, "Why? My staff does the computer work while I work with the patients. Why would I want to spend my time sitting behind a piece of plastic when I have people to do that for me?" So I kept my distance from the computers in my office.

After running my practice for 22 years, I retired. I had nothing to do and no one to do it with. One day I was invited to speak at Zappos, and I gave a two-day Motivational/Inspirational Workshop. Not long after, I was offered a job to be the Coach.

Why are computers so difficult to understand and hard to install?

On my first day there, I was told that the company was starting a new customer service training program, and every new employee had to go through the process on computers and the phone. My aversion to computers hit me square in the face. Not having touched one since my Macintosh debacle, I was hardly prepared for the class.

When Loren, the program instructor, told me to cut and paste, I actually had no idea what he was talking about. Since there was a workbook for the class, I actually looked for the scissors and glue. Times do change.

I appreciate computers

Since then, I have managed to learn about e-mail, and I write on the computer almost every day, but my skills don't extend much beyond that.

My past experiences had created a bad emotional connection with computers that has been difficult to shake. For me and many others, like my mom and dad, our experiences with computers have been painful. My kids, on the other hand, *love computers.* For younger generations who have grown up with those devices, working with computers is not only easy, it's also fun. My youngest created a PowerPoint presentation for me when he was in first grade; he continues to demonstrate the finer points of my iPhone and he doesn't even have one!

THE COMPANY THAT MADE IT SIMPLE

I always asked myself, "Why is it so hard to work with computers?" Why are there so many cords and attachments?" Even when someone else sets up a computer, it takes a day or so to figure everything out.

There are external speakers, a tower, a monitor, a keyboard, a mouse, and a ton of wires. There are never enough plugs, even with a power strip! Who would make something so complex? Do companies that make computers have a Vision that says: "*Let's make products difficult to use, and make them separate, and also make them susceptible to viruses that can ruin all data, and, oh, yeah, let's make them bulky and heavy with as many cords as possible.*" It sure seems like it.

Along came Apple. We just got one the other day. My wife took the computer out of the box, set the monitor up, and plugged it in, placed the keyboard on the counter, and put the remote mouse next to it. Done in five minutes. Only one cord to plug in. We don't need external speakers, a heavy computer tower, no mouse cord, no power strip, no anything else. And, oh yeah, no viruses.

How come all of the billion-dollar computer companies didn't figure this out long ago? It boggles my mind. Deeply rooted in Apple's Culture is Steve Jobs's declaration that Apple products shouldn't need an instruction manual, they should be intuitive and easy to use.

Maybe that's why Apple is doing better than its competition. The user's or customer's experience is the best in the business. Even the Styrofoam packing is a work of art. Apple's simple, easy-to-use, elegant products spark an emotional reaction and create an emotional connection that makes it easy for customers to love them and remember them. The company has fully transformed itself from a sales business to a re-order business and has tons of loyal, enthusiastic fans.

What is your customer's user experience?

User experience is getting more attention.

In many companies, the user experience (UX) is like to putting lipstick on a pig; it comes way too late in the process. UX is important from the beginning. It has to be part of the Vision and the Purpose of the company—built into the thoughts, decisions, and actions of the employees who touch the product before it is finished.

Remember, there are great emotional connections and bad ones. People love you (or your company) or hate you (or your company). Either way, they're loyal: if they love you, they can't get enough, and if they hate you, they stay as far away as possible.

Extra, extra, tweet all about it (reprise)

You should always be asking yourself, "What are we doing that is in the WOW category and that creates a great experience and emotional connection? What retains employees and keep customers coming back?

I first met Bill when he toured Zappos with his daughter, Ellie. A serial entrepreneur, Bill now wanted to start a company with his daughter; it was to be her business, called coffee.org. Bill knew about creating good experiences, and he made sure that's what went into coffee.org. If an order is in before 4:30 in the afternoon, the product is on the truck that night. No waiting until tomorrow. They make things happen!

Bill let me know that they have more than 65 percent repeat customers. Of course, I teased him and said he was slacking compared to Zappos' 75 percent. But we had a good laugh, because we're both confident that he will get there.

We have stayed in touch, and he and Ellie have implemented in coffee.org many of the strategies that are described in this book. They don't just have coffee.org; they also have an online coffee shop where they communicate with their customers. They have made such a great emotional connection with their customers on their Facebook page that they have well over 100,000 "likes."

Now that's creating relationships and treating people like they matter. The company is doing so well that they recently opened up Herbaltea.com. Stay tuned!

WE WANT AN EMOTIONAL CONNECTION THAT ATTRACTS EMPLOYEES AND CUSTOMERS

We want our staff and our customers to love us. If that happens, and we keep it up, we will have loyal employees and customers who attract even more employees and customers.

We've all heard people say, "I love this place . . . that restaurant . . .

this doughnut . . . that person . . . this company." We love these things because they make us feel good.

If you create an experience that makes employees and customers feel great, you have won the battle. You have elicited an emotion and kicked off the process of retaining their love and attraction. Everything you have read in this book is about directing your efforts to providing the best experience possible.

Experience is what it's all about

Here are a couple of definitions to keep in mind in our Information Age:

Experience is the "marketing" of the future. Remember, if you make a customer's experience the best, there is no need for customer service per se.

Experience is what we love to remember—or it's what we want to forget.

Immediate avoidance

When we have a bad experience with food, often just the smell can take us back to an unpleasant moment. If we ordered chow mein and got ptomaine, we usually never order that dish again. Our reaction is reflexive. We don't need to think about why we feel the way we do or how it all started; it just happens.

Avoidance over time

Say you love a restaurant until what you loved about it—the flavor of a dish, the décor, or the service—starts to slip. Your emotional connection will also start to wane, since the place is not delivering the experience that you are used to. *Experience always trumps service!* Perhaps you used to get a favorite table, and now it is hit-and-miss. Or they seem to be taking better care of new customers than you.

You return less and less often, until one day you do not want to go at all. In the end, your experience trumps everything else. Even if the service remains good, if the food is bad or the atmosphere degrading, that's the overall experience you remember.

Zappos understands this. There are no time limits on calls at Zappos. Employees can take as long as needed to help customer find what they need or provide assistance to them.

> **This kind of service is what it's all about. When you're doing the right thing, the right things happen.**

Everyone matters. Even if someone is not your customer, he or she could be. And if they *are* your customers, recognize that they are helping give you a job, so you better do all you can to serve them, and serve them well.

> **Service can be trumped by a poor experience, but great service can help the overall experience be much better.**

The story of Pearl

Here is a story about customer service that created a great experience.

December 20, 2005, was a humid night by Las Vegas standards, and at 6:17 in the evening, a call came in. It was one of thousands handled daily, but this one was unforgettable.

The sweet, quiet voice on the other end of the phone belonged to Pearl. She had seen a certain pair of shoes on the website, and she had questions: How did the shoes fit? Was there another brand of shoes that would be kind to her feet, which had spent too many hours on a hard factory floor?

The Zappos representative sensed that what Pearl really wanted was to talk to someone, even if that someone was a stranger on the other end of the telephone line, so that's what she did. The

There are no limits to great customer service and experience.

rep understood her customer's true desires and responded brilliantly. The rep knew that Pearl was a real person and that she mattered.

The Zappos rep didn't "handle" the call; she took care of the person. That phone conversation helped make the world a better place, for her and for Pearl. And though Pearl never bought anything, she got what she called for: someone to talk to.

The conversation lasted 4 hours and 12 minutes.

Here's the critical question: What emotional connections are you and your company ready to make?

Conclusion

A Few Things to Keep in Mind

This book hasn't exactly been conventional, but it's certainly a product of the Information Age. I'm constantly receiving questions on Facebook, LinkedIn, e-mail, you name it, from people all over the world who want to know more about how to deliver "WOW" for their customers and employees. The notion of saying "Yes!" and delivering "WOW" is, believe it or not, a subject of a worldwide interest. Let me share just one exchange that came from Tim in Russia via Facebook.

> David, hi!
> I'd appreciate very much, if you could share few words about what it meant to "deliver wow" at Zappos for our new group members in "wow-club" Russia.

> Tim,
> Here are a few things to keep in mind:
> · Do whatever you would do for your best friends or family members.
> · Do things in such a way that all they can say is "WOW!"
> · Buff people out royally.
> · Treat them like they matter.
> · Underpromise and overdeliver. If you do that, not only will you be making someone's day, month, or year, but that experience will keep them coming back to you.
> · Trust the process.
> By the way, I have a book coming out in 2013 about this. Keep in touch, and I can send you a copy and if there's enough demand, we can make a Russian translation.
> Best of luck, Brother Love

All I could do was say "No"

During my years at Zappos, many visitors told me how much they liked our Culture and asked me if I had a list of similar companies in their state or city, because they wanted their son or daughter to be able to work for them. Such a company, they hoped, would take good care of their child and allow him or her to reach their full potential.

Regretfully, all I could say was "No." Because when it came to companies with a culture as empowering as Zappos', I knew of a couple, but I certainly had no list to pass along. That is one of the reasons I have written this book: to help companies create their own unique and empowering Culture and to be able to let the world know where they are and what they are all about.

So now it's time for you and your team to get going . . . to create the best Culture on the planet!

It's all about taking people's lives and companies to the Next Level, while making the world a better place.

Acknowledgments

A special thank you to Nick—the Founder and Visionary—Fred, Alfred, Tony, Matt, Galen, Jerry, Pam, Sean, Dr. Hsieh, Keith, and all the rest of my teammates at Zappos. If it weren't for your focused determination to create something great, there wouldn't be a Zappos.

I would also like to acknowledge:

Dr. Charles Ward, who taught me the Unique/WOW Factors and that businesses should be run to maximize their potential;

Dr. Schofield, who helped me understand that I not only had to get off my butt, but that I had to get out of my own way;

Tom Mendoza, for helping me understand that behind a great business success there can also be a great person;

Two sports coaches, Fred Opezzo and Ron Moser, who showed me that extreme mental and physical training will always take you to the top;

And Bob Owen, who taught me that the world is bigger than the neighborhood I grew up in.

Index

About the Author

Dr. David "Doc" Vik is known as The Culture King for promoting his Vision and Purpose: "To Empower People and Companies" throughout the world.

His Culture techniques and strategies yield net results in many different business sectors by attracting and retaining high-quality, engaged employees and loyal customers, while allowing companies to grow at unprecedented rates.

Prior to penning *The Culture Secret*, Doc held the role of coach at Zappos.com, where he helped to empower the employees and drive the Culture. During Doc's tenure, Zappos received worldwide attention for their Culture, including features on *60 Minutes* and *Dateline*, and an elevation of their standing on *Fortune* magazine's list of "Best Places to Work," from #23 in 2009, to #15 in 2010, to #6 in 2011. Before joining the team at Zappos, Doc founded and directed one of the most successful chiropractic clinics in the United States.

Doc began his career in service at the age of fifteen, as the night manager at Taco Bell in Palo Alto. In his spare time, he likes to think and write, spend time and play sports with his family, remodel houses, exercise, cook, golf, and watch golf.